The College Aid Quandary

Dialogues on Public Policy

The presentations and discussions at Brookings conferences and seminars often deserve wide circulation as contributions to public understanding of issues of national importance. The Dialogues on Public Policy series is intended to make such papers and commentary available to a broad and general audience. The series supplements the Institution's research publications by reflecting the contrasting, often lively, and sometimes conflicting views of elected and appointed government officials, other leaders in public and private life, and scholars. In keeping with their origin and purpose, the Dialogues are not subjected to the same formal review procedures established for the Institution's research publications. Brookings publishes the contributions to the Dialogues in the belief that they are worthy of public consideration but does not assume responsibility for their objectivity and for the accuracy of every factual statement. And, as in all Brookings joint publications, the judgments, conclusions, and recommendations presented in the Dialogues should not be ascribed to the trustees, officers, or other staff members of the Brookings Institution.

The College Aid Quandary:
Access, Quality, and the Federal Role

LAWRENCE E. GLADIEUX

ARTHUR M. HAUPTMAN

THE BROOKINGS INSTITUTION/THE COLLEGE BOARD
Washington and New York

Copyright © 1995 by

THE BROOKINGS INSTITUTION
1775 Massachusetts Avenue, N.W., Washington, D.C. 20036

LIBRARY OF CONGRESS CATALOGING-IN-PUBLICATION DATA:

Gladieux, Lawrence E.
   The college aid quandary : access, quality, and the federal role /
Lawrence E. Gladieux, Arthur M. Hauptman.
      p.   cm.
   Includes bibliographical references.
   ISBN 0-8157-3167-1 (pbk. : alk. paper.)
   1. Student aid—United States.   2. Federal aid to higher
education—United States.   3. Student loan funds—United States.
I. Hauptman, Arthur M.   II. Title.
   LB2337.4.G54   1995
   378.3'0973—dc20   95-39067
                                                                          CIP

9 8 7 6 5 4 3 2 1

Typeset in Palatino

Composition by Harlowe Typography, Inc.,
Cottage City, Maryland

Printed by Kirby Lithographic Co.,
Arlington, Virginia

The Brookings Institution

The Brookings Institution is an independent, nonprofit organization devoted to nonpartisan research, education, and publication in economics, government, foreign policy, and the social sciences generally. Its principal purposes are to aid in the development of sound public policies and to promote public understanding of issues of national importance. The Institution was founded on December 8, 1927, to merge the activities of the Institute for Government Research, founded in 1916, the Institute of Economics, founded in 1922, and the Robert Brookings Graduate School of Economics, founded in 1924.

The Institution maintains a position of neutrality on issues of public policy to safeguard the intellectual freedom of the staff. Interpretations or conclusions in Brookings publications should be understood to be solely those of the authors.

The College Board

Founded in 1900, the College Board is a national membership association of schools and colleges whose aim is to facilitate the transition of students to higher education. Serving high schools, colleges, universities, students, and parents, the organization is a nationally recognized source of essential services and information in the areas of assessment, guidance, admission, placement, financial aid, curriculum, and education research. The philosophical core of the College Board is a commitment to educational excellence and equity for all students, and that commitment is embodied in all of its programs and services.

Foreword

The second half of the 1990s could be pivotal in the evolution of U.S. postsecondary education, a large and complex system shaped decisively by federal and state aid. From the opening of the 104th Congress in 1995 through 1998, when the Higher Education Act (the enabling statute for federal student aid) is scheduled to be reauthorized, many decisions will be made about the future of this system. Meanwhile, 30 million students—a substantial part of an entire generation—will attend some form of postsecondary education based on choices influenced by federal policy.

The exact shape the upcoming debate will take is not yet clear. President Clinton came into office committed to reforming student aid; some of his reform proposals were enacted in 1993, while others are pending or have been scaled back. With new Republican majorities in both the House and Senate, the entire domestic policy agenda is in flux, and federal aid to education could be significantly retrenched and restructured.

In such a time, citizens and professionals concerned with postsecondary education in the United States have a responsibility to offer clear, objective advice on ways the present student support system works and should be preserved, as well as where it needs improvement. Federal aid to higher education has achieved much in the half-century since the 1944 GI Bill shaped postwar American society; and since passage of the landmark Higher Education Act in 1965, which has assisted two generations of students in realizing college opportunities. Policymakers need ideas and options for strengthening this system to improve the quality of life for all Americans and provide skills the nation needs for economic vitality into the twenty-first century.

American colleges and universities remain the envy of the world: year after year foreign nationals in record numbers come to study in them. But how well are these institutions serving America, and how effectively is the nation spending scarce resources on postsecondary education? Will low- and moderate-income Americans be able to afford higher education in the future, or will the tuition spiral put a college education beyond the reach of all but rich or upper-middle-income families? What is government's responsibility for assuring the afford-ability and quality of higher education? How well are current federal aid programs working? Should there be different types of financing for students in postsecondary vocational and traditional academic pro-grams? Are there alternatives to the traditional aid programs that might work better for academically high-risk students? And how might federal and state postsecondary education finance policies be more closely linked to maximize quality and access?

Such questions were addressed at a November 1993 seminar spon-sored by the newly formed Brown Center on Education Policy of the Brookings Institution. At that seminar, which was designed to help the Clinton administration formulate policy directions in the area of postsecondary student finance, thirty economists, social scientists, policy experts, and representatives from the Department of Education and the White House reviewed a background paper by Arthur Haupt-man, "Thinking About Next Steps for Reforming Federal Student Aid."

The College Board then joined efforts with the Brown Center to widen the discussion and publish the results. On October 26, 1994, the College Board and the Brown Center convened a group of one hundred fifty individuals, including representatives of College Board member colleges and universities. Discussion centered on another working paper, "Improving Public Policies to Help Students Pay for College," and a series of policy questions developed by Lawrence E. Gladieux and Arthur M. Hauptman. This book is based on that paper and the proceedings of the October 1994 conference.

Lawrence E. Gladieux is executive director for policy analysis of the College Board; Arthur Hauptman is a consultant who has published widely on higher education finance. The authors thank all of the par-ticipants in the October conference who contributed their views and helped shape this publication. An appendix lists the invited speakers, panelists, and other individuals attending the conference. Jacqueline King provided valuable research assistance and helped organize the conference, Roberta Merchant assisted with graphics production and meeting arrangements, Norman Turpin designed the book, and Debra

Shapley and Stephanie Selice provided editorial expertise. Sandy Baum, André Bell, David Breneman, George Chin, Martin Kramer, James Mingle, Thomas Mortenson, and Jane Wellman formed an advisory group that helped guide the project. Lois Rice fostered the Brookings/College Board partnership that made the conference and this publication possible, and Anita G. Whitlock provided administrative assistance for the Brown Center.

The views expressed in this book are those of the individual contributing authors and conference participants and should not be ascribed to the persons or organizations acknowledged above, or to the trustees, officers, or other staff members of the Brookings Institution or the College Board.

Bruce MacLaury
President
The Brookings Institution

Donald M. Stewart
President
The College Board

Contents

xi

Tables

Introduction

A Dutch scholar studying U.S. higher education, Frans J. de Vijlder, recently concluded:

> Postsecondary education funding in the United States is like a landscape in which architects from successive eras have constructed roads, viaducts, and buildings, each in their own style. Some features have been demolished, altered or incorporated into new structures but generally, once something has been built, it remains standing; and the longer something has been part of the landscape, the more it appears to be a permanent feature. This has important advantages, one of which is the variety thus created in the landscape. There is something for everyone. Another advantage is the fact that those who live and work in this environment feel at home because their surroundings are familiar ones which have developed in accordance with the traditions and cultural patterns of successive generations.
>
> However, to think and to act in this way in periods of rapid change, an unstable environment and an uncertain future also has disadvantages . . . the need for more radical changes in the financing mechanisms is becoming ever more urgent. Opinions are divided on what direction change should take, however, and the multiplicity of the parties involved makes it difficult . . . to reach a consensus.[1]

Leave it to a European observer to capture the essence of an American policy dilemma.

De Vijlder is not alone in being struck by the diversity of the American system. In all countries, educational costs must be borne by taxpayers, students, parents, and private donors in some combination. But no other country approaches our crazy quilt of prices, subsidies,

FIGURE 1. *Who Pays for College?*

Percent

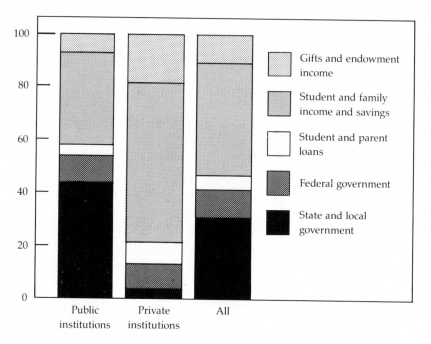

Source: Data for table 2.
Note: Data for these estimated shares are for 1990–91.

and assistance programs for financing higher education, and nowhere else is the cost burden so widely distributed among public and private sources. The untidiness of such a system is both its strength and its perplexity.

American taxpayers provide about two-fifths of the total national investment in higher education, students and their families pay close to one-half, and the rest comes from assorted private gifts and endowments. Figure 1 and tables 1 and 2 provide an approximation of how the total bill is distributed, with separate estimates for public and private nonprofit higher education.[2]

As the figure and tables show, states are the largest government investor, mostly in the form of operating support to public colleges and universities, with some direct aid to students to help meet their costs at both public and private institutions. By comparison the federal

TABLE 1. *Cost of Higher Education: Institutional Expenditures and Student Living Expenses, 1990–91*

	Millions of dollars			Percent		
	Public	Private	Total	Public	Private	Total
Tuition and fees	15,258	22,176	37,434	16.6	54.7	28.3
Student living expenses	26,642	8,743	35,385	29.0	21.5	26.7
Government operating subsidies	43,047	2,110	45,157	46.9	5.2	34.1
Gifts and endowment	6,773	7,548	14,321	7.4	18.6	10.8
TOTAL	**91,720**	**40,577**	**132,297**	**100.0**	**100.0**	**100.0**

Sources: Tuition and fees, government operating subsidies, gifts and endowment: U.S. Department of Education, National Center for Education Statistics, *Digest of Education Statistics 1993*, tables 318, 319, 328, and 329.

Student living expenses: *The College Board Annual Survey of Colleges 1992* and estimated data. Data in this table were weighted by enrollment and by estimated residency patterns to reflect the variable expenses of the average student in each sector of higher education.

TABLE 2. *Who Pays for College: Revenue by Source, 1990–91*

	Millions of dollars			Percent		
	Public	Private	Total	Public	Private	Total
State and local government	39,908	1,362	41,270	43.5	3.4	31.2
State and local appropriations	39,058	374	39,432			
Student grants	850	988	1,838			
Federal government	9,432	4,049	13,481	10.3	10.0	10.2
Federal institutional support	3,989	1,736	5,725			
Student grants	4,173	1,173	5,346			
Student loan subsidy	1,270	1,140	2,410			
Student and parent loans	3,809	3,419	7,228	4.2	8.4	5.5
Student and family income and savings	31,798	24,199	55,997	34.7	59.6	42.3
Gifts and endowment income	6,773	7,548	14,321	7.4	18.6	10.8
TOTAL	**91,720**	**40,577**	**132,297**	**100.0**	**100.0**	**100.0**

Sources: State and local appropriations, federal institutional support, gifts and endowment income: U.S. Department of Education, National Center for Education Statistics, *Digest of Education Statistics 1993*, tables 195, 318, 319, and 358.

Federal student grants, federal student loan subsidy, student and parent loans: The College Board, *Trends in Student Aid: 1984 to 1994* (New York, 1994).

State student grants: 1990–91 National Association of State Scholarship and Grant Programs survey.

Student and family income and savings: Residual based on total cost of education and living expenses.

Notes on Tables 1 and 2:

Tables 1 and 2 present an approximation of the national investment in higher education and the shares of the total cost borne by state and local governments, the federal government, private donors, students, and families. Many factors complicate such an estimation, so much so that previous attempts at a similar accounting have produced widely varying results. (See, for example, Martin Kramer, *Background Papers and Reports*, National Commission on Responsibilities for Financing Postsecondary Education [Washington, April 1993]; Arthur M. Hauptman, *Background Papers and Reports*, National Commission on Responsibilities for Financing Postsecondary Education [Washington, April 1993]; and Thomas G. Mortenson, "Purchasing Power of the Pell Grant Maximum 1973–74 to 1993–94," *Postsecondary Education OPPORTUNITY*, vol. 12 [April 1993], p. 10.)

In this analysis, we have attempted to capture the total amount spent on student attendance in higher education, including student living expenses as well as instructional costs. Table 1 presents these costs as the sum total of what colleges charge (tuition and fees), what subsidies are received from government and private philanthropy that reduce the price of tuition to something less than the true operating costs of institutions, and what students pay to live while they are enrolled.

The data on tuition and fees are straightforward, but the figures on government subsidy are more complex. The data for state and local support include only appropriations. We excluded grant and contract income because it generally supports specific projects and does not contribute to the general revenue of institutions. In the case of federal expenditures, however, we combined appropriations with an estimate (30 percent) of the amount of federal research spending that contributes to the general operating expenses of institutions, such as faculty salaries, upkeep of libraries and physical plant, and training of graduate student researchers. This estimate is based on the average indirect cost rate paid by the National Institutes of Health (NIH).

Estimating student living expenses is also problematic. Colleges and universities annually report room and board charges to the Department of Education, but these figures omit many other costs associated with paying for college, such as transportation, books, and supplies. Using room and board data alone, moreover, would assume falsely that the majority of students live either on campus or in off-campus housing that closely approximates the cost of on-campus accommodations. According to the Department of Education, less than 20 percent of students reside on campus. More than half live off campus in housing other than their parents' home, and most of this latter group are older students who are less likely to share an apartment near campus than younger students.

The College Board conducts a more comprehensive annual survey of college costs, including room and board on and off campus, books and supplies, transportation, and a catch-all category of "other expenses." The figures are drawn from the student budgets that colleges develop for purposes of awarding financial aid. A drawback of using such data is that, aside from the on-campus room and board figures, institutions vary in how they estimate the other cost components and what they recognize as legitimate student expense.

The approach we have taken here is to use the College Board's data from its 1990–91 survey of colleges and, where possible, to weight these data by the Department of Education's figures on student housing status. The result is a hardly perfect but plausible approximation of aggregate student living expenses.

Table 2 estimates who pays how much of the total costs presented in table 1. Some of the information from table 1, such as gifts and endowment income, is simply carried over to table 2. The state and local and federal categories, however, break down government operating subsidies into major components.

"State student grants" and "federal student grants" report, wherever possible, only the share of these funds that are spent at public and private nonprofit institutions. Likewise, the "student and parent loans" figures include only borrowing for nonproprietary institutions. The subsidy value of federally sponsored student loans, estimated at 25 percent of the amount borrowed, is included in the federal share. The balance of loan volume is included under "student and parent loans."

The category "student and family income and savings" is a residual figure. It is the amount of the total cost remaining once the other revenue sources have been taken into account. This figure is substantially higher than the estimates of other analysts. Our inclusion of living expenses boosts the overall student and family share (including income and savings as well as the repayable, non-government contributes a relatively small share of the total costs of the postsecondary education system. Yet historically federal support has been strategic in key areas of national importance. In two types of spending today—sponsored research and student financial aid—federal outlays far exceed those of the states and private sources. These federal commitments grew out of two post–World War II public agendas: cold war competition in science and defense technology on the one hand, and the movement for civil rights and equal opportunity on the other.

Our focus in this book is the policy stream that has given rise to federal programs providing $30 billion a year to help students and families close the gap between their ability to pay and the costs of college attendance. Figures 2 and 3 and tables 3 and 4 show the growth and changes in the mix of student aid over the past three decades, from federal as well as state and institutional sources. In real dollar terms, the total amount of aid available to students grew more than 15–fold between 1963–64 and 1993–94, largely because of the expanding federal role. While institutions supplied almost half of all aid at the beginning of this period, they provided less than one-fifth in 1993–94. The federal government currently generates three-fourths of the total. Less than one-third of the federal amount comes in the form of direct expenditures; the balance is in the form of federally sponsored loans to students and their parents. As shown in figure 3, federal grants more than doubled as a percentage of all aid between 1963–64 and 1973–74, but have since receded in relative importance, contributing less of the total in 1993–94 than in 1963–64.

The prospects for government support of higher education in the mid-1990s are far from good in either Washington or the state capitals. In the states, economic recovery has not brought a resurgence of fund-

---

subsidized value of loans) to nearly 40 percent for public higher education and 70 percent for private higher education.

Some might contend that this accounting overestimates the total cost and that students would face many of the same living expenses whether or not they were students. Others might propose that opportunity costs, or foregone income, be included as part of student expenses. A case can be made that, especially for low-income students, the cost of foregone income is a very real consideration. We sought instead as complete an accounting as possible of out-of-pocket costs in a given year.

There are as many ways to approach such a cost accounting as there are analysts who might take on the task. The merit of the one presented here is that it provides as thorough an approximation of total costs of attendance as the available data permit.

FIGURE 2. *Amount of Aid to Postsecondary Students, 1963–93*

Billions of dollars

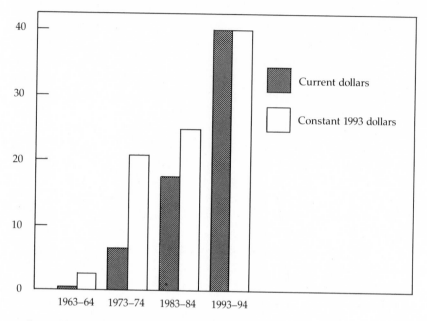

Source: The College Board, *Trends in Student Aid: 1984 to 1994* (New York, 1994).

ing for higher education; other priorities, like health care and prisons, increasingly divert state tax resources. Tuition at public institutions in most states continues to rise to help fill the revenue gap for higher education.

In Washington, the outlook is hardly brighter as efforts to downsize government, spin off functions to the states, balance the budget, and reduce taxes promise hard times ahead for most federal domestic programs. Yet federal student aid has long enjoyed a wide base of political support. Giving people an equal chance through education (regardless of their economic and social origins) is too much a part of the American promise, too imbedded in our public values, to be crowded off the national agenda. Some level of national or direct federal responsibility will likely continue to be accepted in the principal areas of federal activity affecting higher education—sponsored research as well as student aid.

FIGURE 3. *Composition of Aid to Postsecondary Students, 1963–93*

Percent

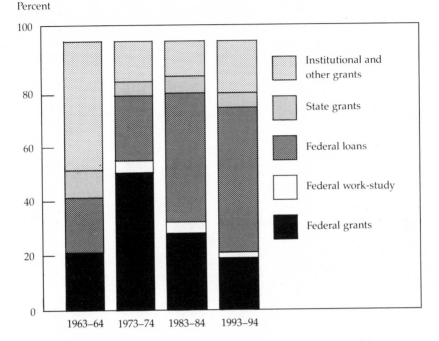

Source: The College Board, *Trends in Student Aid: 1984 to 1994.*

Precisely what level of investment, however, remains to be seen. Since 1980, the real value of government aid to students has grown but has not kept pace with tuition and related charges. Prices charged by both public and private institutions have consistently run ahead of inflation, family incomes, and available student assistance in the 1980s and 1990s. With the 1994 elections, it is now possible that there will be not just erosion but substantial retrenchment at the federal level.

In a climate of extreme uncertainty about government commitments, proponents of the existing aid programs surely need to mobilize to argue for investment, to resist draconian policy changes, and to stem the policy drift toward a system that places more and more of the cost burden on students and their families.

At the same time, it is strategically important for educators to present options where the present aid system needs improvement or restructuring. Student aid delivery has become an enormously com-

TABLE 3. *Aid Awarded to Postsecondary Students, 1963–64 to 1994–95, in Millions of Current Dollars*

	1963–64	1971–72	1973–74	1975–76	1977–78	1979–80	1981–82	1983–84	1985–86	1987–88	1989–90	1991–92	1993–94	Preliminary 1994–95
Federally supported programs														
Generally available aid														
Pell grants	0	0	50	937	1,588	2,505	2,299	2,792	3,567	3,736	4,768	5,777	5,652	5,650
SEOG	0	153	189	201	244	333	362	361	410	419	445	498	564	554
SSIG	0	0	0	20	60	76	78	60	76	75	71	62	72	73
CWS	0	240	296	295	469	595	624	683	656	635	663	760	771	760
Perkins Loans	114	312	433	460	615	646	580	682	703	805	903	868	919	972
Ford Direct Student Loans	0	0	0	0	0	0	0	0	0	0	0	0	0	1,737
Family Education Loans	0	1,274	1,139	1,267	1,737	3,926	7,219	7,576	8,839	11,385	12,151	13,993	21,182	22,936
Subsidized Stafford	0	0	0	0	0	0	(7,150)	(7,260)	(8,328)	(9,119)	(9,508)	(10,805)	(14,123)	(14,104)
Unsubsidized Stafford	0	0	0	0	0	0	0	0	(0)	(0)	(0)	(0)	(2,033)	(7,139)
SLS	0	0	0	0	0	0	(15)	(148)	(269)	(1,830)	(1,835)	(2,022)	(3,477)	(32)
PLUS	0	0	0	0	0	0	(54)	(168)	(242)	(436)	(808)	(1,165)	(1,550)	(1,660)
SUBTOTAL	114	1,979	2,107	3,179	4,712	8,081	11,161	12,155	14,251	17,060	19,007	21,963	29,160	32,681

Specially directed aid													
Social security	0	570	784	1,093	1,370	1,587	1,996	220	0	0	0	0	0
Veterans	67	1,320	2,261	4,180	2,700	1,821	1,351	1,148	864	762	790	876	1,192	1,410
Military	42	59	80	97	104	167	232	297	342	349	364	394	405	421
Other grants	9	20	33	63	82	114	106	62	67	92	110	160	168	186
Other loans	0	51	62	45	42	42	109	279	372	303	361	372	456	405
SUBTOTAL	117	2,020	3,221	5,478	4,299	3,731	3,793	2,005	1,646	1,502	1,620	1,796	2,221	2,423
Total federal aid	231	3,999	5,328	8,657	9,011	11,812	14,954	14,160	15,897	18,562	20,627	23,759	31,382	35,104
State grants	56	269	364	490	677	788	921	1,106	1,311	1,503	1,719	1,968	2,375	2,665
Institutional and other grants	270	942	1,009	1,169	1,228	1,460	1,746	2,280	2,962	3,808	4,951	6,679	8,233	9,057
TOTAL FEDERAL, STATE, AND INSTITUTIONAL AID	557	5,210	6,701	10,316	10,916	14,060	17,621	17,545	20,169	23,873	27,297	32,406	41,990	46,826

SEOG = Supplemental Educational Opportunity Grants; SSIG = State Student Incentive Grants; CWS = College Work-Study; SLS = Supplemental Loans for Students; PLUS = Parent Loans for Undergraduate Students.

Source: The College Board, *Trends in Student Aid: 1985 to 1995* (New York, 1995).

Note: Before 1992, loans from the Family Education Loan Program were referred to as Guaranteed Student Loans or Stafford Loans.

TABLE 4. *Aid Awarded to Postsecondary Students, 1963–64 to 1994–95, in Millions of Constant 1994 Dollars*

	1963–64	1971–72	1973–74	1975–76	1977–78	1979–80	1981–82	1983–84	1985–86	1987–88	1989–90	1991–92	1993–94	1994–95 (Preliminary)
Federally supported programs														
Generally available aid														
Pell grants	0	0	154	2,433	3,653	4,650	3,520	3,955	4,866	4,786	5,570	6,199	5,731	5,570
SEOG	0	536	584	522	560	618	554	511	559	537	520	535	572	546
SSIG	0	0	0	51	137	142	119	85	103	97	83	67	73	72
CWS	0	840	915	766	1,079	1,105	955	968	895	814	775	815	782	749
Perkins Loans	531	1,092	1,339	1,195	1,415	1,199	888	966	959	1,031	1,054	931	932	958
Ford Direct Student Loans	0	0	0	0	0	0	0	0	0	0	0	0	0	1,712
Family Education Loans	0	4,460	3,522	3,292	3,996	7,288	11,052	10,730	12,056	14,584	14,196	15,015	21,480	22,613
Subsidized Stafford	0	0	0	0	0	0	(10,947)	(9,896)	(11,360)	(11,681)	(11,108)	(11,594)	(14,321)	(13,906)
Unsubsidized Stafford	0	0	0	0	0	0	(0)	(0)	(0)	(0)	(0)	(0)	(2,061)	(7,039)
SLS	0	0	0	0	0	0	(23)	(202)	(367)	(2,344)	(2,143)	(2,170)	(3,526)	(32)
PLUS	0	0	0	0	0	0	(83)	(229)	(330)	(559)	(944)	(1,250)	(1,572)	(1,637)
SUBTOTAL	531	6,929	6,515	8,260	10,841	15,002	17,089	17,216	19,439	21,854	22,206	23,567	29,571	32,221

Specially directed aid														
Social security	0	1,995	2,424	2,840	3,152	2,946	3,056	312	0	0	0	0	0	0
Veterans	313	4,621	6,991	10,861	6,212	3,380	2,068	1,625	1,178	976	923	940	1,209	1,390
Military	195	208	249	251	240	310	355	421	467	447	426	422	411	415
Other grants	41	70	103	164	189	212	162	87	92	118	128	171	170	184
Other loans	0	179	191	117	97	78	166	395	508	388	421	399	462	400
SUBTOTAL	549	7,073	9,959	14,233	9,890	6,926	5,807	2,840	2,245	1,924	1,892	1,927	2,252	2,388
Total federal aid	1,080	14,001	16,473	22,493	20,731	21,928	22,896	20,056	21,684	23,778	24,098	25,494	31,823	34,610
State grants	262	942	1,126	1,273	1,558	1,463	1,410	1,566	1,788	1,926	2,008	2,112	2,408	2,628
Institutional and other grants	1,260	3,297	3,120	3,036	2,825	2,710	2,674	3,229	4,040	4,878	5,784	7,166	8,349	8,929
TOTAL FEDERAL, STATE, AND INSTITUTIONAL AID	2,602	18,240	20,719	26,803	25,114	26,100	26,979	24,851	27,511	30,581	31,890	34,772	42,580	46,167

SEOG = Supplemental Educational Opportunity Grants; SSIG = State Student Incentive Grants; CWS = College Work-Study; SLS = Supplemental Loans for Students; PLUS = Parent Loans for Undergraduate Students.

Source: The College Board, *Trends in Student Aid: 1985 to 1995*.

plicated system heavily driven by federal legislation and rules. Everybody agrees the system needs to be made more readily accessible and predictable for students, parents, and administrators who must negotiate its complexities. Issues of equity in need-based distribution patterns must be constantly reviewed, as do issues of quality control and cost-effectiveness. To the extent that policy objectives are sharpened and the system made more coherent, the federal aid programs will be in a stronger position to compete for scarce resources.

In that spirit the College Board and the Brown Center on Education Policy brought together one hundred fifty policymakers, analysts, and practitioners in October 1994 to review the design and purpose of federal student assistance and to consider policy alternatives. We expected no ready consensus but did hope to spark constructive debate, which was certainly achieved. This publication grows out of the working paper prepared for that discussion and the contributions of the conference participants. Likewise, we hope this book generates constructive debate that will ultimately lead to better public policy supporting both equity and quality in higher education.

Chapter 1 traces the evolution of federal postsecondary aid policies and then reviews the themes and performance of the federal assistance programs. This is relatively recent history and only occasionally intersects with the state role in higher education. Unlike other policy arenas (welfare or interstate highways, for example) where federal and state programs have been systematically linked in some fashion, the federal and state governments are often like ships passing in the night when it comes to higher education. An ongoing challenge for policymakers is how to mesh federal and state efforts better to strengthen the crazy quilt of postsecondary finance.

Chapter 2 identifies a series of key policy questions on the structure and direction of the federal student assistance effort and then reports the main lines of debate when these questions were posed at the October 1994 conference.

We conclude in chapter 3 by capturing salient points of divergence and agreement at the conference and suggesting guideposts for future reform.

NOTES

1. Frans J. de Vijlder, *Financing Higher Education in the United States* (Leiden/ Zoetermeer: Ministry of Education of The Netherlands, 1994).

2. The cost and revenue accounting presented here is for public and independent, nonprofit institutions of higher education. Comparable and reliable statistics for the independent, for-profit or proprietary sector of postsecondary education are not available. However, we do know that proprietary schools typically receive no operating support from government, do not raise money from foundations or alumni, and are therefore far more dependent on tuition than most nonprofit institutions. But their students are substantially subsidized through the federal government's grant and loan programs. At some proprietary schools, up to 90 percent of tuition is paid by federal student aid. (See Richard W. Moore, "Proprietary Schools and Direct Loans," *Select Issues in the Federal Direct Loan Program* [U.S. Department of Education, 1994], pp. 13–24.) According to 1992–93 data from the National Postsecondary Student Aid Study, more than 70 percent of students in proprietary schools receive financial aid, and most of these students receive only federal, not state or institutional, aid. By comparison, 60 percent of students in private nonprofit schools receive aid, usually from a mix of federal and nonfederal sources. At public four-year institutions, 45 percent receive aid; at public two-year ones, 27 percent.

Chapter 1

A Fifty-Year Retrospective on Federal Student Aid Policy

The democratization of college opportunities in the United States can be traced through two centuries—from the land grant college movement and the establishment of state universities in the nineteenth century, to the GI Bill, establishment of community college systems, and explosion of enrollments following World War II. Major phases in the growth of higher education have extended access to new groups in society.

It is in the past several decades, however, that equal opportunity has become a centerpiece of public policy toward higher education. A principal expression of this goal has been the growth of need-based student assistance. Today the federal government is by far the largest sponsor of such aid; the establishment of this federal commitment, however, did not come easily.

MILESTONES

1944. The Servicemen's Readjustment Act, or GI Bill, was enacted by Congress to reward veterans who had served their country during wartime and help them catch up with their peers whose lives had not been interrupted by military service. During the 1940s and 1950s, GI Bill benefits extended higher education opportunities to thousands of men and women who otherwise might never have gone to college.

But advocates of broader federal support for higher education unrelated to military service faced an uphill struggle. In fact, aid-to-education proposals of all kinds repeatedly ran aground in Congress, blocked by civil rights and church-state controversies and fear of federal control of education. Moreover, the idea of federal scholarship support, whether based on financial need or academic merit, met resistance from those who believed students should not get a free ride.

Many members of Congress at that time had worked their way through college.

1958. The Soviet launch of Sputnik finally gave Congress the opportunity to justify a limited form of student assistance in the name of national security. The National Defense Education Act of 1958 provided low-interest loans for college students, with debt cancellation for those who became teachers after graduation. The law also established graduate fellowships to encourage students in the sciences, mathematics, engineering, and other strategic fields. Outright scholarships or need-based grants for undergraduate study, however, were still considered beyond the pale.

1965. The Kennedy legacy, the civil rights movement, and the Johnson administration's war on poverty converged in the mid-1960s to break new ground. The 89th Congress presided over the broadest sweep of social legislation since the New Deal. Along with breakthroughs in civil rights came large-scale aid to education, including the Higher Education Act (HEA) of 1965.

Title IV of HEA embodied the first explicit federal commitment to equalizing college opportunities for needy students. This goal was to be advanced through need-tested grants that were not linked to academic ability, and through student support programs such as Upward Bound (initially part of the war on poverty legislation of 1964) and Talent Search, designed to identify and foster access for college-able students who were poor. Colleges wishing to receive an allocation of funds under the new Educational Opportunity Grants program were required to make "vigorous" efforts to identify and recruit students with "exceptional financial need." Title IV of the law also included College Work-Study (another program first ushered in as part of the war on poverty) to subsidize employment of needy students, and the guaranteed student loan (GSL) program to ease the cash-flow problems of middle-income college students and their families.

The impetus for the GSL program was mounting support in Congress for a tuition tax credit for parents with children in college. Advocates of greater access for needy students worried that enactment of a tax credit and the resulting loss of federal revenue would hurt chances of funding new programs for low-income students under HEA. The loan program appeared to be a much less costly way to help the middle class, especially since it relied on private sources of loan capital. At least initially, the program was not expected to draw heavily from the federal Treasury, so that federal resources could be focused primarily on the neediest students.

1968. Congress reauthorized HEA three years later with only slight modifications. A new program, Special Services for the Disadvantaged, was added to the law; in combination with Upward Bound and Talent Search, they came to be known as the TRIO programs.

Although the ballooning costs of the Vietnam conflict constrained the growth of many domestic programs, appropriations for student aid grew rapidly in the late 1960s. These monies eclipsed other forms of federal support for higher education, such as construction of academic facilities.

1972. The next reauthorization rounded out the principal programs and the basic charter of today's federal student aid system.

During the debate leading up to this legislation, the higher education community urged Congress to enact formula-based, enrollment-driven federal aid to institutions. But legislators decided that funding aid to students was the more efficient and effective way to remove financial barriers for needy students and thus equalize opportunities in higher education. Congress also viewed student aid as a way to harness market forces for enhancing the quality of higher education. Students, voting with their feet, would take their federal aid to institutions that met their needs; less satisfactory institutions would wither.

Congress made a further point in the 1972 legislation by substituting the term "postsecondary education" for "higher education" and broadening the range of options available to students. The intent was to break the stereotype that education beyond high school meant full-time attendance in a four-year academic program leading to a baccalaureate degree. In keeping with this theme, the 1972 HEA amendments extended greater federal recognition and support to career and vocational education, community colleges, and trade schools, as well as to students in part-time programs.

Above all, proprietary schools gained full eligibility to participate in the programs under Title IV of the act. Over the next two decades, these schools would proliferate and prove uniquely adept at capturing federal student aid dollars.

Congress also expanded the types of assistance available to students. The Nixon administration had proposed Basic Educational Opportunity Grants to replace three existing federal student aid programs administered through the colleges: Educational Opportunity Grants, National Defense Student Loans, and Work-Study. Congress refused to repeal the campus-based programs but did adopt Basic Grants (now called Pell Grants), envisioning this new program as a foundation for all forms of aid and one that students would apply for directly to the federal government. Initially authorized at a maximum of $1,400, the intent of Basic Grants was to provide a minimum level of resources to help assure access to higher education; the campus-based programs would provide supplemental aid to help assure student choice among programs and institutions.

State Student Incentive Grants were also authorized in 1972. The SSIG program provided federal matching dollars to induce states to enact or expand their own need-based student grant programs. The 1972 law established the Student Loan Marketing Association (Sallie Mae) as a publicly chartered private corporation to increase liquidity and capital availability in the GSL program.

1976. Issues of quality control surfaced in the next reauthorization debate; Congress may have had second thoughts about some of the educational options that had been legitimized in 1972. But Congress was more concerned about getting banks to lend money for postsecondary education. The 1976 amendments provided federal incentives for states to establish loan guarantee agencies.

Another significant expansion of the aid system was authorized with the addition of a few words to the statute. Students without high school degrees became eligible for federal assistance so long as they had the "ability to benefit" from postsecondary training.

1978. In an off year of the reauthorization cycle, but under pressure for some kind of response to the perceived middle-income squeeze in financing college costs, Congress passed the Middle Income Student Assistance Act (MISAA) of 1978. As in 1965, tuition tax credit proposals had built up another head of steam in Congress. To head them off, congressional Democrats and the Carter administration developed a counterproposal to widen eligibility for Pell Grants and open subsidized guaranteed loans to any student regardless of income or financial need.

1979. A year later Congress passed a little-noticed amendment assuring banks a favorable rate of return on guaranteed student loans by tying their subsidies directly and fully to changes in Treasury bill rates. (Previously the rate had been set by a group of government officials with a cap on how much lenders could receive.) With the economy moving into a period of double-digit inflation and interest rates, student loan volume—and associated federal costs—exploded. The problem of lender participation and capital shortage in the loan program became a thing of the past.

1980. The pressure to expand financial aid for the middle class continued through the reauthorization of 1980. Outmaneuvering the Carter administration as well as the congressional budget committees, the education authorizing committees further liberalized criteria governing need-tested aid programs yet shielded the open-ended GSL program from measures to curb eligibility, reduce subsidies, or otherwise control ballooning federal costs. The 1980 legislation also created offshoots of the GSL program providing supplemental borrowing opportunities for parents of dependent undergraduate students and for students who were financially independent of their parents.

1981. However, the legislative expansion of 1980 was short-lived. Ronald Reagan was elected president, and domestic social programs faced a budgetary onslaught in the early 1980s. Many provisions of the 1980 reauthorization were repealed in the 1981 budget reconciliation, need was reintroduced as a condition of eligibility for guaranteed loans, and an origination fee of 5 percent was imposed on borrowers as a cost-cutting measure.

The growth curve in federal student aid leveled off sharply in the first half of the 1980s. Grant support dropped, as did the overall purchasing power of student aid. Loan eligibility and subsidies were trimmed; but as an entitlement that had become popular with the middle class, the GSL program proved the most resilient form of aid. Loan volume continued to grow, although at rates slower than between 1978 and 1981.

1986. In the mid-1980s, in the face of continued Reagan administration threats to the programs, congressional advocates of student aid adopted a damage control strategy. A reauthorization that was basically status quo was the result. Legislators voiced concern about the increasing reliance of students on loans, but they came up with no effective remedies to combat this trend as tuition at both public and private institutions spiraled well above inflation. Federal borrowing ceilings were increased.

1987–90. Loan volume shot up again after the 1986 reauthorization. Meanwhile, media attention and public concern focused on mounting student loan defaults and proprietary trade school abuse. Through the annual budget reconciliation process, Congress forced a series of changes aimed at reducing defaults and effecting other cost savings.

1992. Leaders of the reauthorization process in Congress again said they wanted to achieve a better balance between grant and loan support for students, boosting grant aid and reducing reliance on loans. But the 1992 legislative outcome continued the policy drift in the opposite direction.

The prospect of a post–cold war peace dividend had fueled hopes that Pell Grants might be turned into an entitlement or mandated spending program with automatic annual increases for inflation. But the peace dividend never materialized, leaving no room under the budget rules for such an expansion.

After the attempt to create a Pell entitlement failed, Congress followed the path of least resistance by boosting dollar ceilings for the loan programs. In addition to raising the borrowing limits for students, Congress uncapped the parent loan (PLUS) program, thus allowing parents to borrow up to the total amount of school costs minus any other funds the student might have received. In estimating the federal costs of all the new borrowing authority, House and Senate sponsors assumed that low market-interest rates would continue, thus minimizing the projected expense of the changes and avoiding any violation of spending caps mandated in the budget process.

The 1992 legislation also created a new, unsubsidized loan option not restricted by financial need. This was designed to make loans available to those Americans in the middle-income range who had been squeezed out of eligibility for the subsidized guaranteed loan. ("Unsubsidized" means that the government does not pay interest costs while the borrower is in school.)

This legislation further established a consolidated federal methodology for determining student and family ability to pay that applies to all Title IV programs, not just Pell Grants. The net impact of the new methodology (which many states and institutions also use as the basis for awarding their own funds) is a dramatic reduction in expected family and student contributions, extending potential eligibility for aid (particularly loans) to a substantially larger portion of middle-class Americans.

Like the response to the 1978 and 1986 legislation, student loan volume has once again ballooned as a result of the 1992 reauthorization. Increased loan limits, introduction of unsubsidized loans, and changes in need analysis boosted student and parent borrowing to more than $25 billion in 1994–95, a $10 billion increase in just two years.

The 1992 legislation also authorized a small demonstration program to test the feasibility and cost effectiveness of the federal government administering student loans directly through postsecondary institutions as an alternative to guaranteeing loans through private banks. Finally, Congress in 1992 sought to tighten oversight of institutions participating in federal aid programs by redefining the responsibilities of the gatekeeping triad—the Department of Education, postsecondary accreditation bodies, and the states. The principal new thrust placed more reliance on states through the creation of state postsecondary review entities (SPREs) to help determine institutional eligibility under Title IV.

1993. Even as Congress hammered out the 1992 legislation, presidential candidate Bill Clinton was on the campaign trail promising a complete overhaul of the student aid system if he was elected. He repeatedly cited defaults, excessive bank fees, high government costs of the loan program, and the aid system's overall lack of effectiveness in making college affordable. Emphasizing the responsibilities of those who receive aid, Clinton called for benefits that students could earn through community service or reimburse at rates geared to their future income.

A year later, in fact, President Clinton won congressional passage of the Student Loan Reform Act of 1993, altering the way student loans are financed, originated, serviced, and repaid. The 1993 legislation greatly expanded on the direct loan demonstration program authorized in 1992, calling for at least 60 percent conversion of federal student loan volume from guaranteed to direct lending over a five-year period. The act also called for more flexibility in how borrowers repay, including an income-contingent plan that calibrates monthly repayments to a percentage of the borrower's income for up to 25 years.

In his first year in office, the president also won passage of a national and community service program, though on a much smaller scale and with much less of a link to the student aid system than he had called for during the campaign. As enacted and funded, the national service corps provides benefits to only a tiny percentage of federal student aid recipients.

1994. Having made student aid reform a top domestic policy commitment, and having won early legislative victories to support plans in this area, the Clinton administration struggled to fulfill another campaign promise—to streamline the regulatory process for student aid programs. Yet to implement the host of legislative initiatives passed in both 1992 and 1993—everything from SPREs to direct lending and income-contingent repayment—the Clinton Department of Education ultimately generated more than 70 rule-making packages. The volume and complexity of the new rules as well as contention with the education community over many of them led to a sense that the regulatory process was as overwhelming as ever.

At the same time, the Clinton administration sought to project a longer-range, Phase II agenda of student aid reform. The Department of Education held regional hearings around the country to test reactions and gather ideas on how federal aid might be further restructured, better targeted, and simplified. However, the administration's Phase II vision sparked little enthusiasm among student aid administrators coping with the broad scale of change already under way, or with college leaders preoccupied with the administration's SPRE proposals. The administration's Phase II designs were also overtaken by events, namely the 1994 election.

1995. With new Republican majorities in both the House and Senate, the policy environment in Washington became as unsettled as it had been since the early 1980s. The federal commitment to education and other domestic social programs once again hangs in the balance. The Republican Contract With America calls for dramatic downsizing of the federal government, devolution of many functions to the states, a moratorium on federal regulations, tax relief for the middle class— and a balanced budget by the year 2002. A contentious debate has begun on the role and scope of government and the division of responsibilities between Washington and the states.

In the Reagan years, the momentum and will for change persisted for about two years. By 1983, for example, the administration had abandoned plans to abolish the Department of Education and a variety of other proposals for restructuring and retrenching the federal establishment. Economic recession and tough political realities had tempered the Reagan revolution. Of the original Reagan budget blueprint for the 1980s, the proposed tax cuts were fully phased in, but spending cuts fell far short of targets needed to offset lost tax revenue. The result was a $4 trillion national debt by the end of the decade, a fiscal legacy that continues to cast a long shadow over policymaking in the 1990s.

The outcome of today's hectic debate is anyone's guess. The only certainty is that almost everything government does—and how it should be done—is on the table. Most student aid funds come from the discretionary part of the federal budget; therefore, student aid tends to be especially vulnerable in the search for cost savings. Some programs will surely be eliminated, others cut back.

In the case of the lone student aid program that operates as an entitlement—federally sponsored loans—the fine print of the Contract With America proposed removing the in-school interest subsidy, which means students would have to pay interest (or let it accrue to their loan principal) while they are enrolled in school. Such a change, it is estimated, would save $10 billion over five years. Intense lobbying by students and higher education officials, however, appears to have blocked this cut. Instead, Congress is considering a patchwork of fees and reduced payments for banks, students, state guarantee agencies, and institutions to achieve required savings in the budget reconciliation process.

Meanwhile, the Clinton student aid reforms legislated in 1993 could be eclipsed by the Republican agenda. The 104th Congress will likely slow, if not reverse, the Clinton administration's conversion from guaranteed to direct student loans; and the Clinton community and national service plan may be substantially cut back if not eliminated. Republicans may also blunt another Clinton reform theme—tighter quality control and gatekeeping for institutions participating in Title IV programs. Colleges have complained loudly that the Clinton rules implementing the 1992 oversight provisions fail to target problem schools and are unreasonably onerous for institutions doing a good job of stewarding federal funds. The Republican call for deregulation has resonated for many in higher education, even as the budget-cutting agenda has sent shock waves through this community.

But all these issues pale in comparison with the far-reaching implications of changes that would result from applying the block-grant concept to student aid delivery. Some congressional leaders and governors have called for consolidating student aid as well as job training funds into block grants to the states that would then be controlled by state policymakers.

Finally, the perennial issue of tuition tax credits (this time advanced by the Clinton administration) has worked its way back into the federal policy fray. President Clinton's "middle-class bill of rights," a counter to Republican tax cut proposals, includes a proposed tuition tax credit of up to $10,000 for families earning $100,000 or less. Once again, tax breaks are being offered as a policy to help students and their families pay for college.

POLICY DRIFT

A half-century after the first GI bill, three decades since the establishment of federally guaranteed students loans, and more than two decades after the creation of a national basic grant program, both the central commitment to federal support for higher education and the mechanisms of such support are under full-scale attack. This is therefore an important time to take stock of these government policies— how they have evolved over time and what they have accomplished.

What has changed since the principal federal aid programs of today were first legislated? The aid system has indeed become a "landscape" with overlays of "roads" and "viaducts" from different eras, as the Dutch scholar Frans J. de Vijlder noted. Many originally chance features now seem permanent and familiar, especially to professionals in higher education. There *is* "something for everyone" in the complexity of the current system.

In one sense, not a great deal has changed. The strategy Congress adopted in the early 1970s of granting and lending to students rather than institutions has become the financial aid system's hallmark. Today more than 90 percent of U.S. Department of Education funds for postsecondary education are in the form of student financial aid. In fact, with additions and elaborations the same programs are in place as those established more than a quarter-century ago.

Underlying policies, however, have shifted. On many counts, today's aid system looks much different from what the early legislative framers envisioned.

Growing Reliance on Loans

Above all, the drift toward a system that relies primarily on student debt to finance higher tuition has turned the original commitment to equal opportunity on its head. The legislation of the 1960s and early 1970s established a commitment to help disadvantaged students through need-based grant programs, while helping middle-class families through government-guaranteed (but minimally subsidized) private bank loans.

Today, loans are far and away the largest source of aid, even for the lowest-income students. Since the mid-1970s when student borrowing began to grow, loans have increased from about one-fifth to more than half of all available student aid. Federally sponsored loans provided more than $25 billion in 1994–95, over four times the size of the Pell Grant program that was meant to be the system's foundation.

Over the long haul, the Clinton student loan reforms could help redress the loan-grant imbalance. Part of the intent of direct lending from its conception has been lower federal costs compared with the elaborate subsidy structure of the guaranteed loan program. At this writing, the shift to direct lending—and the projected cost savings— are being challenged by the Republican Congress. To the extent that the direct lending program does survive and savings do result, more federal resources could become available for investment in Pell and other grant aid. On the other hand, direct lending could lead to more borrowing; to the extent that it succeeds in streamlining delivery of loans, it may make loan capital that much more accessible and attractive.[1]

Erosion of Need-Based Standards

Meanwhile, the antipoverty origins of the 1960s legislation have faded into history as eligibility for federal student aid has been extended up the economic ladder. This development has been doubleedged. On the one hand, the broadening of eligibility has popularized programs with the middle class and therefore strengthened the programs' political base. The stronger political foundation resulting from the middle-income legislation of 1978 probably helped to protect these programs from what could have been worse cutbacks in the early 1980s. On the other hand, the shift has diluted the federal emphasis on subsidies for low-income students and led to the predominance of loans in the mix of available aid.

The changes in need analysis enacted in 1992 have produced another expansion in middle-income eligibility, inflating officially recognized need by several billion dollars. But with no corresponding increase in available funds, more "need" is chasing roughly the same number of available dollars. The probable effect is that scarce dollars have shifted up the income scale, at the expense of more disadvantaged students and families.

Growth in Self-Supporting Nontraditional Students

In the past several reauthorizations, Congress has also sought to adjust aid policies to better meet the needs of older and part-time students. The original programs and procedures of need analysis were designed for families with dependent children who attend college full time. However, growing numbers of students are beyond the traditional age group, attend less than full time, and have ongoing family and work responsibilities while in school. Over the past two decades, the proportion of postsecondary students over age 25 has roughly doubled, from one-fifth to two-fifths of all students. Students qualifying as independent or self-supporting under federal rules now constitute a substantial majority of Title IV aid recipients.

How the government should support such students has become an ongoing policy concern in the 1990s. In 1992, Congress liberalized eligibility for some categories of independent and part-time students but sharply restricted it for single independent students. Policymakers remain concerned that the aid system is insufficiently sensitive to the wide-ranging circumstances of an increasingly diverse postsecondary population. At the same time, trade-offs are involved. Outside of entitlement programs, expanding eligibility for independent adult students potentially reduces the dollars available to dependent students from low-income families.

Use of Aid for Short-Term Vocational Training

When Congress decided to "broaden the mainstream" of postsecondary education in the early 1970s, no one had envisioned the burgeoning of the proprietary trade school industry. The proprietary sector has been highly responsive to federal student aid policies. It flourished in response to the postwar GI Bill; once fully eligible for programs under Title IV of the Higher Education Act, the industry again expanded rapidly in the late 1970s and 1980s. Entrepreneurs created hundreds of new for-profit schools and programs during this period, all enrolling aid-eligible students, many of them focusing on low-income, inner-city areas. Alongside training traditionally offered by the proprietary sector in secretarial work and business, refrigeration, welding, auto mechanics, and the like, new programs sprouted offering training for truck drivers, security guards, retail clerks, and nannies.

By the late 1980s proprietary school students received one-fourth of Pell Grant funds and more than one-third of guaranteed loan volume. Program abuse and disproportionately high default rates in the trade school sector, however, attracted mounting publicity, prompting a series of legislative and regulatory remedies. The trade school industry and its share of federal student aid funds have since contracted significantly. Proprietary schools nonetheless continue to have a major stake in federal aid. Of roughly 7,500 institutions now eligible for the Title IV programs, about 4,000 are proprietary. Students at these institutions currently receive one-sixth of all Pell Grants and one-tenth of all guaranteed loans.

Compared with 1970, when perhaps 2,000 collegiate institutions participated in federal student aid programs, today's regulatory dilemma for the Department of Education is the sheer number and diversity of schools and the kinds of education and training supported by Title IV. A focus on short-term vocational training fits with the national agenda of retraining and upgrading the skills of the work force. But student aid is not necessarily the most effective mechanism for financing such training. There is also virtually no coordination of Title IV aid with the substantial amount of support for postsecondary employment training provided by other federal programs and agencies.[2]

Use of Aid for Remediation

Over time, more and more federal student aid dollars have been provided to students who are not prepared to do college-level work. This trend toward funding remediation has occurred for two reasons.

First is the "ability to benefit" provision added to the law in 1976, which allowed hundreds of thousands of non–high school graduates to qualify for Title IV aid. The standards used to determine which students can benefit have been low and largely unregulated. For a long time, the tests were developed and administered by the schools to which the students were applying. More recently, a variety of federally sanctioned independent tests have been in use. However, the "passing grade" has been low enough to allow all but a handful of students to qualify for aid on this basis.

The second reason for the trend toward Title IV funding of remediation is simply the inadequate preparation of large numbers of high school graduates. The ongoing debate over K-12 school reform and standards underscores the fact that too many high school graduates cannot yet do college-level work. In recognition of this underpreparedness, the existing federal student aid legislation allows students taking remedial courses to receive federal aid for up to one year of coursework. But the regulations governing this limitation are unclear on how eligibility is to be terminated, and many students taking remedial work continue to receive aid for periods longer than one year.

THE SYSTEM'S ACHIEVEMENTS AND SHORTFALLS

The above historical review suggests that the objectives, mechanisms, and constituencies of federal student aid today are considerably more diffuse and complex than they were a quarter-century ago. Thus gauging the impact and success of aid policies over this period is far from cut-and-dried, and the indicators presented here will only scratch the surface of such an evaluation. Federal student aid clearly has been an important force in shaping postsecondary education in the post–World War II era. Though causes and effects are arguable, the various federal student aid efforts no doubt helped fuel a half-century of explosive growth in college attendance and educational attainment by Americans.

In 1940, American college and university enrollments totaled 1.5 million. A decade later, with the postwar influx of GI Bill beneficiaries, enrollments had increased by 60 percent to 2.4 million. When the Higher Education Act passed in 1965, enrollments had doubled to nearly 6 million. In the mid-1990s, American colleges and universities enroll 15 million students: one and one-half times the number enrolled thirty years ago, five times the enrollment of the Korean War era, and ten times pre–World War II levels. This growth in student enrollment far exceeds growth in the U.S. population. Meanwhile, the proportion of the population 25 to 29 years old who have completed at least four years of college has quadrupled since 1940.

Federal student aid has surely had something to do with producing such gains in enrollment and attainment and in creating the diversity of today's college student population. Yet one casualty over time has been naive expectations about what might be accomplished through student aid to advance national goals of educational equity, quality, and affordability. The balance of this chapter examines these goals and indicators of progress toward them over recent decades.

Changes in Access and Attainment

Table 5 shows the increase in college participation rates over the past two decades. Among high school graduates, more than three-fifths now enter college in the fall following their graduation, up from less than half in 1973. As table 5 also shows, this increase in college participation has been widespread. The increase in enrollment rates was not limited to two-year colleges; enrollment rates in both two- and four-year colleges increased substantially. Among high school graduates from families in the bottom fifth of the income distribution, enrollment rates doubled between 1973 and 1992.

Table 6 presents a broader statistical picture of progress in educational attainment. The proportion of all persons 25 to 29 years old who have completed at least four years of college nearly doubled over the past thirty years, from 12.4 percent in 1965 to 23.7 percent in 1993 (though most of this increase occurred by 1980). The educational attainment of women improved much more than for men—not surprising, as it was 60 percent lower in 1965. Another encouraging trend is that the educational attainment of blacks also nearly doubled in the same period.

Notwithstanding such advances, the problem of unequal opportunity has proved more intractable than anyone anticipated in the early years of the Higher Education Act. In the late 1960s and early 1970s, widely cited reports from the Bureau of the Census showed that a college-age youth from a family with an income over $15,000 was

TABLE 5. *Percent of Recent High School Graduates Enrolled in College, by Type of College, Family Income, and Race and Ethnicity, 1973–92*

October	Type of college			Family income			Race and ethnicity		
	Total	2-year	4-year	Low	Medium	High	White	Black	Hispanic
1973	46.6	14.9	31.7	20.3	41.0	64.4	n.a.	n.a.	n.a.
1974	47.6	15.2	32.4	n.a.	n.a.	n.a.	48.7	40.5	53.1
1975	50.7	18.2	32.6	31.2	46.2	64.5	49.1	44.5	52.7
1976	48.8	15.6	33.3	39.1	40.5	63.0	50.3	45.3	53.6
1977	50.6	17.5	33.1	27.7	44.4	66.3	50.1	46.8	48.8
1978	50.1	17.0	33.1	31.4	44.3	64.2	50.4	47.5	46.1
1979	49.3	17.5	31.8	30.5	43.1	63.4	50.1	45.2	46.3
1980	49.3	19.4	29.9	32.5	42.7	65.2	51.5	44.0	49.6
1981	53.9	20.5	33.5	33.6	49.3	67.6	52.4	40.3	48.7
1982	50.6	19.1	31.5	32.8	41.7	71.7	54.2	38.8	49.4
1983	52.7	19.2	33.5	34.6	45.4	70.2	55.5	38.0	46.7
1984	55.2	19.4	35.8	34.5	48.4	74.0	57.9	39.9	49.3
1985	57.7	19.6	38.1	40.2	50.7	74.5	58.6	39.5	46.1
1986	53.8	19.3	34.5	33.9	48.4	71.4	58.5	43.5	42.3
1987	56.8	18.9	37.9	36.9	49.9	74.0	58.8	44.2	45.0
1988	58.9	21.9	37.1	42.5	54.7	72.8	60.1	49.7	48.5
1989	59.6	20.7	38.9	48.1	55.4	70.9	61.6	48.0	52.7
1990	60.1	20.1	40.0	46.7	54.5	76.5	63.0	48.9	52.5
1991	62.5	24.9	37.6	39.5	58.4	78.2	64.2	47.2	52.5
1992	61.9	23.0	38.9	40.9	56.9	80.9	n.a.	n.a.	n.a.

Source: U.S. Department of Education, National Center for Education Statistics, *The Condition of Education 1994*, p. 40.

Note: Low income is defined as the bottom 20 percent of all family incomes, high income as the top 20 percent of all family incomes, and middle income as the 60 percent in between.

n.a.: Not available.

nearly five times more likely to be enrolled in higher education than one from a family with an income of less than $3,000.[3] The new student aid programs were to be on the cutting edge of policy to close such gaps.

Today college-age young people from the highest-income range ($75,000 or more by Census categories) are over three times more likely to be enrolled in college as those from the lowest income groups (under $15,000 in the Census categories).[4] Though shifts in the distribution of income probably invalidate a precise comparison of Census data over the intervening decades, these figures suggest a measure of im-

TABLE 6. *Percent of Persons Ages 25 to 29 Who Have Completed Four Years of College or More, 1940–93*

	1940	1950	1965	1970	1975	1980	1985	1990	1993
All races									
Both sexes	5.9	7.7	12.4	16.4	21.9	22.5	22.2	23.2	23.7
Male	6.9	9.6	15.6	20.0	25.1	24.0	23.1	23.7	23.4
Female	4.9	5.9	9.5	12.9	18.7	21.0	21.3	22.8	23.9
White									
Both sexes	6.4	n.a.	13.0	17.3	22.8	23.7	23.2	24.2	24.7
Male	7.5	n.a.	16.4	21.3	26.3	25.5	24.2	24.2	24.4
Female	5.3	n.a.	9.8	13.3	19.4	22.0	22.2	24.3	25.1
Black									
Both sexes	1.6	2.9	6.8	7.3	10.7	11.6	11.5	13.4	13.2
Male	1.5	2.4	7.3	6.7	11.4	10.5	10.3	15.1	12.6
Female	1.7	3.2	6.8	8.0	10.1	12.5	12.6	11.9	13.8
Hispanic origin									
Both sexes	n.a.	n.a.	n.a.	n.a.	8.8	7.7	11.1	8.1	8.3
Male	n.a.	n.a.	n.a.	n.a.	10.0	8.4	10.9	7.3	7.1
Female	n.a.	n.a.	n.a.	n.a.	7.3	6.9	11.2	9.1	9.8

Source: U.S. Department of Commerce, Bureau of the Census, *Educational Attainment in the United States: March 1993 and September 1993*, Current Population Reports P20-476 (Washington, 1993), table 18.

n.a.: Not available.

provement in access to college opportunities during this period. But the more certain point is that large gaps in educational opportunity stubbornly persist.

A variety of other statistics confirm the continued socioeconomic disparities in access to and successful completion of higher education programs. Among recent high school graduates, those from low-income families are still half as likely to enroll in college by the fall following their graduation as those from high-income families (see table 5.) The enrollment rate of recent black high school graduates (47 percent in 1991) still lags behind that of whites (64 percent); the 1991 rate for Hispanic high school graduates was 53 percent.

Moreover, without the vast expansion of two-year community colleges in the postwar period, these gaps in enrollment would no doubt be substantially larger. The longer view of educational attainment presented in table 6 underscores this point. In 1993, whites ages 25 to 29 are still twice as likely to have completed four years of college as blacks and three times more likely than Hispanics.

Such gaps in opportunity, and the failure of student aid to close them, should not really come as a surprise. As we have noted, the targets of federal student aid today are more diffuse and complex than they were at the outset. In its conception, federal student aid was primarily about helping those who otherwise might not have access to higher education. In their evolution, federal policies have become as much (or more) about relieving the economic burden for those who would probably pursue postsecondary programs without such aid.

We also know more today about the complexity of the college-going process. Enrollment and success in higher education are functions of many factors—academic aptitude and prior schooling, family and community attitudes, motivation, and awareness of opportunities—not just ability to pay. Above all, there appear to be huge and growing disparities in the capacity of K-12 educational systems to prepare young people for the world beyond high school. Higher education, much less student aid as a financing strategy, cannot by itself redress social deficits and imbalances that appear to threaten our country's future.

Access to What?

The notion that having students vote with their feet would somehow assure quality in the postsecondary education marketplace was a dubious proposition from the start. More than a quarter-century later, it is clear that the marketplace rationale begged important questions of institutional quality and accountability, as well as consumer information, awareness, and protection.

Federal student aid programs have been plagued by institutions that defraud both taxpayers and students, offering programs of little or no educational or vocational value or that are so poorly managed they do not serve students effectively. High student loan default rates, as well as low completion and placement rates for students who receive aid, have reflected these problems and galvanized public concern.

Much of the trouble has come in the for-profit sector; but the baggage of fraud and abuse has encumbered the entire student aid effort and triggered tighter rules affecting all of postsecondary education. In part, this reflects successful lobbying by the proprietary school indus-

FIGURE 4. *Average Undergraduate Tuition and Fees, 1970–94, in Current Dollars*

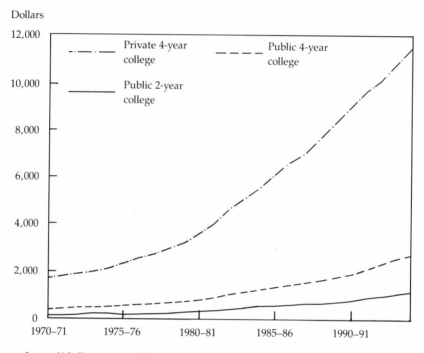

Source: U.S. Department of Education, *Digest of Education Statistics: 1994* (Government Printing Office, 1994), table 304.

Note: 1994 figures are estimates.

try, which has blocked proposals to remove trade schools from Title IV or authorize separate regulatory controls over them. It also suggests that policymakers are not necessarily persuaded that all problems relating to consumer protection and lax educational standards are in the noncollegiate sector. Policymakers are increasingly prone to be more critical in examining the effectiveness and performance of traditional higher education as well.

From the beginning, federal student aid policy has been shaped by a commitment to access. The legacy of access to higher education is deeply ingrained in our public values. Debates over student aid policy have typically centered on whether policy changes would hinder or expand access for disadvantaged students. But we have learned that

FIGURE 5. *Average Undergraduate Tuition and Fees, 1970–94, in Constant 1994 Dollars*

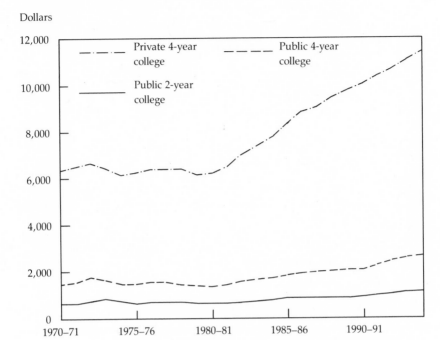

Dollars

Source: U.S. Department of Education, *Digest of Education Statistics: 1994*, table 304.
Note: Constant dollar figures were calculated using the consumer price index for all urban dwellers (CPI-U).

access does not assure quality; in fact, access can ill serve students if they do not complete their education or graduate without the skills they need to succeed.

Low-income, at-risk students are actually the *most* ill served when student aid incentives encourage their enrollment in programs subject to minimal quality control. In such programs they have, at best, only modest chances of success; at worst, they are left with no job, a defaulted loan, and a bad credit record.

The history of federal student aid suggests that future policies need to strike a better balance between the goals of access and quality. "Access to what?" rather than "access no matter what" should guide policymaking.

FIGURE 6. *Cost of Attendance at Public Institutions as a Share of Family Income, 1975–92*

Percent

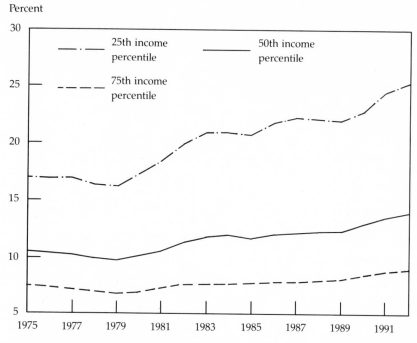

Source: U.S. Department of Education, National Center for Education Statistics, *The Condition of Education 1994* (Washington, 1994), table 8-1.

Affordability

In the 1970s, family income levels increased faster than tuition; growth in student aid outstripped both tuition increases and growth in the number of eligible students; and grant aid was more common than borrowing.

All these trends, however, turned against college affordability in the 1980s and 1990s. Family income has generally remained flat and has been far outpaced by tuition increases, which at both public and private four-year institutions have averaged at least twice the rate of inflation since 1980. Figures 4 and 5 show, in current and constant

FIGURE 7. *Cost of Attendance at Private Institutions as a Share of Family Income, 1975–92*

Percent

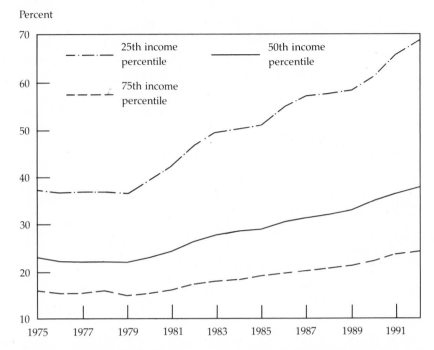

Source: U.S. Department of Education, National Center for Education Statistics, *The Condition of Education 1994*, table 8-1.

dollars, average undergraduate tuition and fees from 1970 through 1994. Tuitions have risen annually by more than 8 percent in the last fifteen years, while annual growth of the consumer price index has averaged about 4 percent. Public sector prices have increased most sharply in the 1990s, rising at three times the rate of inflation as the economy and tax revenues in most states have declined.

Another perspective on college affordability is provided in figures 6 and 7, which trace the cost of attending public or private institutions as a share of family income between 1975 and 1992. The share of income required to pay for higher education generally declined in the 1970s but has risen since 1980. Figures 6 and 7 also show that since 1980 the already great disparity between low- and high-income families in the percentage of income needed to pay college costs has widened even further, reflecting the growth of income inequality over the period.

Student aid, meanwhile, has failed to close the gap between family income and college costs. The real value of total aid available to students has increased since 1980. However, the growth has been primarily in the form of loans and has not kept pace with growth in tuition levels or in the eligible student population.

Table 7 summarizes the trends in costs of attendance, aid, and median family income from 1970–71 to 1992–93. Total aid per full-time equivalent (FTE) enrollment in higher education has grown 5 percent since 1980, whereas median family income has grown only 2 percent. But cost of attendance has ballooned 43 percent in public four-year institutions and 60 percent at private four-year schools.

In the mid-1990s, tuition increases appear to be moderating slightly. According to the College Board's annual survey of colleges, tuition and fees in both public and private four-year higher education rose 6 percent in both 1993–94 and 1994–95, still above the consumer price index but less than the rate of increase of the early 1990s. More and more private institutions worry about pricing themselves out of the market and are trying to restructure their operations to contain costs. In the public sector, economic recovery has for the moment relieved some pressure on tuition increases as a revenue source in state budgets. But the tuition spiral is not likely to end, nor is student aid likely to catch up any time soon.

*   *   *

To say that federal aid programs have fallen short of expectations for achieving broad national goals is surely not to pronounce the effort an abject failure or to encourage those who would decimate the federal commitment in this area. It is, rather, to say that we sorely need constructive debate and proposals to strengthen the system that we have. The foregoing history and assessment set the stage for asking questions essential to any attempt to envision better aid policies in the future.

TABLE 7. *Cost of Attendance, Aid, and Median Family Income, 1970–71 to 1992–93*

Constant 1992 dollars

	Average cost of college attendance			Total aid per full-time equivalent enrollee	Median family income
Year	Private four-year	Public four-year	Public two-year		
1970–71	10,203	5,012	3,746	2,325	33,519
1975–76	10,197	4,919	3,816	3,079	34,249
1980–81	9,069	4,134	3,286	3,086	35,839
1985–86	11,908	4,980	3,847	2,911	36,164
1990–91	13,527	5,493	3,633	3,024	37,950
1992–93	14,514	5,936	3,734	3,256	36,812
22-year change (percent)	42	18	no change	40	10
12-year change (percent)	60	44	no change	6	3

Source: The College Board, *Trends in Student Aid: 1984 to 1994.*

Note: Although full-time equivalent (FTE) enrollment figures are not available for all postsecondary education, dividing the total amount of aid available by FTE enrollments in higher education does provide a rough estimate of how well aid has kept pace with growth in enrollments. It does not reflect substantial growth in proprietary school student participation in student aid in the 1980s.

The large increase in aid per FTE between 1970 and 1975 was due to the commencement of the Pell Grant program and increased GI Bill benefits for veterans after the Vietnam conflict.

NOTES

1. See Martin Kramer, "Policy Implications of Direct Lending," *Select Issues in the Federal Direct Loan Program* (U.S. Department of Education, 1994), pp. 1–12.

2. See Janet S. Hansen, ed., *Preparing for the Workplace: Charting a Course for Federal Postsecondary Training Policy* (National Academy Press, 1994).

3. For example, see *Toward Equal Opportunity for Higher Education,* Report of the Panel on Financing Low Income and Minority Students in Higher Education (New York: College Entrance Examination Board, 1973), p. 11.

4. U.S. Department of Commerce, Bureau of the Census, *School Enrollment—Social and Economic Characteristics of Students: October 1993,* Current Population Reports P20-479 (Government Printing Office, 1993), table 16.

Chapter 2

Toward the Next Century: Focusing the Debate

Chapter 1 traced the evolution of federal student aid policies and programs over the past half-century, noting their accomplishments and problems and identifying a set of policy trends and concerns that cloud the future of this critically important national effort. In chapter 2, we aim to establish a framework for debate that will be useful to policymakers as we approach the twenty-first century.

As evidenced by the 1994 elections, there is no predicting the timing, direction, or speed of pendulum swings in American politics, or how such changes will influence policy outcomes in Washington. The impact of the 104th Congress on federal domestic commitments, including postsecondary student aid, remains to be thrashed out. The next Congress, in 1997–98, is scheduled to consider reauthorization of the entire Higher Education Act; the 106th Congress will lead the country into the next century.

Particular issues ebb and flow on the policy agenda. Our objective here is to bring into sharper focus the fundamental policy questions that will likely persist about the government's role and responsibility in equalizing opportunities for postsecondary education. We have been assisted in this effort by the one hundred fifty people who attended and contributed their thoughts at a conference held at the Brookings Institution in October 1994. What follows are the questions and analysis presented at the conference, along with highlights of the conference discussion. Conferees are for the most part identified by name, though it has not been possible to list every person who expressed one or another opinion.

The conference was organized around three sets of questions. The first concerns whether student aid is the most appropriate vehicle for financing all forms of postsecondary education and training. The second set asks whether the federal government should play a more prominent role in setting academic performance and cost standards than it has previously. The final set examines alternatives for making existing aid programs more effective in raising participation rates.

THE STUDENT AID STRATEGY

IS FEDERAL STUDENT AID AS STRUCTURED UNDER TITLE IV OF THE HIGHER EDUCATION ACT THE MOST APPROPRIATE VEHICLE FOR SUPPORTING ALL FORMS OF POSTSECONDARY EDUCATION AND TRAINING?

The success of student aid as the principal federal strategy for equalizing opportunities for higher education depends on certain essential conditions: first, that students have adequate, accurate early information on which to make their choices; second, that the students who receive aid are adequately prepared to do college-level work; third, that student aid itself does not influence what colleges charge; and fourth, that adequate quality control and consumer protection measures are in place to ensure that the institutions students choose to attend provide education and training of sufficient quality.

These conditions for success, however, have not always been met.

—Many prospective students are unaware of their potential eligibility for aid and are discouraged by the "sticker shock" of rising tuitions.

—A substantial percentage of student aid funds—as much as one-quarter and possibly more—are awarded to students who have not demonstrated they have the skills necessary to do college-level work.

—The availability of student aid does influence the tuition and fees charged by some institutions, particularly trade schools where federal aid often represents a majority of all institutional revenues.[1] The 1992 expansion of loan limits (especially the uncapping of parent loans and the creation of unsubsidized loans for all undergraduates) could exert a similar influence on the pricing behavior of many traditional colleges.

—Finally, high default rates and the fact that most aid recipients (as well as most college students) do not complete their educational programs are two signs that quality control efforts in federal student aid programs are not working as well as they should.

The traditional policy response to these problems has been to modify student aid programs so that they will work better. But it may be time to consider alternatives to the traditional student aid programs for helping individuals in short-term vocational training not leading to a degree, and students who are not currently prepared to do college-level work.

Should the financing of students in short-term, nondegree vocational programs be different from the financing of students in degree-granting programs?

Although millions of individuals in training programs have benefited over the years from the availability of federal student aid, there are at least two reasons to reconsider whether student aid (particularly in the form of loans) is the best way to finance short-term vocational training. First, the default rates on student loans for short-term vocational programs are several times greater than those for academic programs. Second, there is much overlap and duplication between student aid and job training programs; individuals are frequently eligible for both types of assistance, although they typically receive only one.

The way in which nondegree, short-term vocational training is currently financed in this country is confusing to participants and administrators alike. Individuals seeking training are eligible for two distinctly different types of assistance. They may qualify for vouchers in the form of student aid such as grants, loans, and work-study. Or they may participate in training through government contracts with training providers under the Job Training Partnership Act (JTPA), Perkins Vocational Education programs, the School to Work program, Tech-Prep programs, and other federal and state efforts.

Youths and older people in training programs who are not college bound receive more assistance than is commonly understood. According to a study by the National Academy of Sciences, individuals in postsecondary vocational training benefited from roughly $20 billion in federal assistance in 1991, substantially more than the amount spent on student aid for college students.[2] Federal student aid, in fact, is the largest source of support for postsecondary vocational training.[3]

Good arguments can be made that the current overlap in financing mechanisms for short-term postsecondary vocational training should be eliminated or reduced. Focusing on one strategy or the other—vouchers or provider contracts—might allow for a concentration of resources rather than the current diffusion of effort. But neither of these two strategies has clearly met the goal of providing quality training at reasonable cost to the federal government. Thus, in advocating change, it is possible that moving in either direction could result in more ineffective public policies.

Depending exclusively on student aid would increase reliance on loans as the primary means for financing short-term training. An argument in favor of vouchers is that to the extent participants in vocational training receive direct economic benefit from the training, the benefit should be financed in the form of a loan. Consistent with this argument, defaults might be reduced by gearing repayment to the borrower's income once the training has been completed.

The default rates of borrowers in vocational programs, however, suggest it would be unwise to rely even more on loans as the primary source of financing for this type of training, at least until quality control in these programs is substantially improved. Moreover, income contingency only reduces defaults for those who eventually have enough income to repay.[4]

The case for moving to a system of performance-based contracting rests on the notion that this would be a better way to control for quality and costs than simply putting purchasing power in the hands of students through student aid vouchers, whether loans or grants. It would seem that paying providers on the basis of their performance might yield better results than a student aid system that has operated on virtually no performance basis.

However, the experience of the Department of Labor in JTPA and other job training programs does not necessarily support the case for performance-based contracting. These programs have a mixed record of performance in both job placement and program management.

Short of shifting entirely to contracts for job training and apprenticeship as the means for financing short-term vocational training, a more modest reform would be to limit the amount of student aid that the federal government directs to organizations providing the training. One of the most serious abuses in current student aid programs is the pricing strategy of many trade schools, which seeks to maximize the amount of aid their students are eligible to receive. This results in tuitions that often exceed what most people would regard as the reasonable costs of the training. If, instead, the amount of reimbursement were limited to reasonable costs, one of the key elements of contract-based job training could be incorporated into the student aid programs while leaving the structure of student aid in place.

■ Conference Discussion

Janet Hansen began the discussion, speaking from her experience as staff director for the National Academy of Sciences (NAS) study of postsecondary vocational training policy. She said the question about whether student aid was the right mechanism for supporting postsecondary education and training reminded her of what Churchill said about democracy: that it is the worst form of government except any others one could think of. The NAS study committee concluded there are lots of problems with the student aid system but could not identify alternatives that are necessarily any better.

The voucher approach, Hansen said, seems to work well for traditional college students. Given aid and the opportunity to choose, within broad limits, such students can make good choices. But the postsecondary world has expanded to new populations for whom vouchers do not work as well as for traditional students. Whether contracting, based on the job training model, would be a more effective way to support noncollegiate students is unclear. The contract approach assumes a client-caseworker relationship that facilitates a match between clients and programs. But a client-caseworker relationship has not typically been part of postsecondary education.

As for the record of the job training programs, Hansen cautioned that performance contracting can have perverse incentives. This characterized the early years of JTPA, when cost incentives led to "creaming" by contractors—that is, taking only those students with the greatest chances of success and not serving disadvantaged individuals. As Hansen put it: "Incentives work; you get what you pay for," meaning that they can lead to results opposite from what was intended. More recently, she went on to say, JTPA management has been improved and now works much better in serving disadvantaged students, "which is not to say it is exactly right." But it now does have a serious, performance-based approach to funding.

The NAS committee, Hansen said, also wrestled with the am-
biguities of defining what constitutes postsecondary training: Is it
preparing people to enter the workplace, meeting the workplace
training needs of people currently employed, second-chance training for disadvantaged individuals who have gotten off track, or all
of the above? When we talk about job training as a model, she
said, we must remember that job training programs are not necessarily intended for the same population as is postsecondary education. The JTPA and adult basic skill programs are largely aimed
at highly disadvantaged populations, which only sometimes overlap with postsecondary populations.

Maureen McLaughlin of the U.S. Department of Education responded to Hansen's comments by explaining that the Clinton
Administration was grappling with these issues as it has tried to
develop an initiative on work force training. The Departments of
Education, Labor, and Health and Human Services, as well as the
Office of Management and Budget are working together to figure
out the best approach. This interagency process reflects a recognition that there are lots of things going on at the federal level affecting work force preparedness that are not coordinated. Student
aid is by far the largest amount of federal money spent for training
activities, so any discussion of postsecondary training policies has
to include student aid. This is why, in fact, the Department of Education commissioned the NAS study.

To sort out the array of students who need education and training, and the vehicles for providing them, McLaughlin explained
that the Department of Education has drawn up a matrix that di-
vides students both by age and by type of education and training
they are receiving. This two-dimensional grid would divide students into "youths" and "adults" and types of study needed into
basic, college preparatory, short-term, and longer-term training
and education.

Brookings president Bruce MacLaury suggested such a grid
might better be configured in at least three dimensions so that the
type of financing could be included as another variable. A fourth
dimension might be the institutional delivery mechanism. "Before
one can ask whether the currently structured Title IV works or
not," he said, "it would be helpful to think in those matrix
terms. . . . Having made all these boxes, I realize we deconstruct

them immediately by saying there are overlaps. You can't put people in boxes. But I still think analytically, it's better to make the boxes and then see where the overlaps are."

Conferees applauded the Clinton administration's efforts to develop a work force training agenda and rationalize federal policies in this area. The 1990 report, *America's Choice: High Skills or Low Wages!*, was cited to underscore the point that while the United States has the best higher education system in the world, we are not doing as good a job as our competitors in preparing students for the workplace and in linking school with work.[5]

Opinion was divided, however, on goals, delivery systems, and how best to serve disadvantaged populations. Stephen Blair, president of the Career College Association, suggested that "workplace skills are driving today's debate . . . and we are breaking down the distinction between training and education." He further suggested the need to "break the back of this discussion of college," asserting that "80 per cent of the jobs in this country require technical education beyond high school, and 20 per cent require the traditional baccalaureate degree. The vast majority of our people will need technical education, so the question is: How do we as a society provide it? How do we pay for it? And what role do different institutions have in providing it?"

As the principal representative of proprietary schools, most of them offering short-term nondegree training and a few offering bachelor's and graduate degrees, Blair argued that the most important distinction is not institutional type and control, but "what is the most cost-effective way of delivering" the needed training, whether by certificate or degree. And, he argued, there must be accountability, "so consumers know that what they are buying will give them a job in the skill in which they are educated."

In response, other participants were concerned that the greatest problems of quality control and excessive loan default rates appear to be in the proprietary sector: students who pay with their federal dollars and receive no or little training, or who give the schools their aid dollars on the promise of acquiring job skills that later do not translate into jobs or that result at best in minimum-wage employment.

Dolores Cross, president of Chicago State University, suggested a "criterion" of institutional eligibility for Title IV should be whether a proprietary school articulates to "a degree-granting institution"—that is, a two-year associate's or bachelor's degree, "rather than any postsecondary program that leads to a minimum wage." She and others argued it is important to have short-term programs articulate with higher levels of postsecondary training, so students can improve their skills moving from one part of the system to another.

As to default rates, Blair rejoined that his member schools are trying to serve students who are very poor, and "poor people default at a higher rate than nonpoor people. . . . If you make loans the driving factor, and then you turn around and say: You can't have a high default rate, then you will force schools to make the market choice of not serving high-risk students." He added that many of his schools are moving out of the inner cities for this reason. Federal student loans, he argued, remain a sound way to pay for such training, even if a school has a 40 percent default rate. The "return on investment of the 60 percent who make it" justifies the taxpayer cost of the loans.

Maureen McLaughlin argued that this view of balancing the winners and losers and declaring a net gain for society overlooks the fact that those who do not make it are saddled with loan obligations and thus in many cases are more disadvantaged than when they started out. This is one reason the Clinton administration has pushed for an income-contingent repayment option. But more important than anything else, McLaughlin said, is "to figure out how to help more people succeed."

Finally, James Mingle of the State Higher Education Executive Officers Association made the most radical proposal regarding postsecondary training policy: "Take nondegree vocational programs and make them a state responsibility. Then let the states decide whether to support them through vouchers or through contracts on a reasonable cost basis." His argument was that states feel most acutely the economic security requirements for having a well-trained work force of technicians, apprentices, and the like. Public accountability would be strengthened, Mingle said, because "the states would have greater motivation to have only quality providers making students qualify for good jobs." He added that this would follow from the arguments made by Alice Rivlin in *Reviving the American Dream* for shifting federal and state roles to make states responsible for what she called the "local productivity agenda."[6]

Should financial aid, particularly loans, be available for students who are not prepared to do college-level work? Are there alternatives to the traditional student aid programs that might work better for high-risk students?

As a result of the low standards used in determining the ability-to-benefit of students who have not graduated from high school or its equivalent and the low level of preparation of many high school graduates, a substantial proportion of current student aid recipients are not prepared to do college work. A reasonable estimate is that one-quarter or more of student aid dollars are currently spent for individuals who either are not prepared for college or are taking at least one course below the postsecondary level.

To make progress in equalizing educational opportunity, it is critical that individuals who are not presently capable of doing college-level work be able to prepare themselves to benefit from postsecondary education and training. *The policy question is whether the federal student aid programs, particularly loans, are the best way to finance the remediation necessary for such preparation.*

The substantial and growing use of student loans to finance remediation is troublesome. Under existing policies, hundreds of thousands of students who are demonstrably not prepared for college are borrowing thousands of dollars each on the slim chance they will succeed in their programs. Using grants for this purpose may be justified, but using loans as a principal source of funds is like calling a third strike on those at-risk students who are already two strikes down in the count.

One possible alternative to using loans for remediation would be for the federal and state governments to provide basic skills opportunities on a fully subsidized basis, just as a public high school education is available free of charge to all teenagers. Such remediation might be provided at a number of sites where it already occurs, including adult education programs, trade schools, and community colleges, as well as a variety of community-based organizations.

Unlike the student aid programs, however, the organizations that provided the remediation would be paid by the government on the basis of costs associated with remediation, rather than what the institution charges for tuition. Students would not be charged tuition for these services or might only be charged a nominal fee. In addition to not being charged tuition and not having to borrow, students also would benefit because these remediation courses would not count against their future eligibility for federal student aid.

If the organizations that provide remediation were reimbursed on the basis of the costs of providing it rather than the tuitions and other charges that apply to all students, the amount of federal funds expended on such remediation could be less than what is currently spent for the same purpose through student loans.

Expansion of the federal TRIO student service programs would be another non–student aid approach that might be more effective than direct financial assistance in helping students who are not yet ready for college. Although the results and evaluations of the TRIO programs have been mixed, there are enough success stories to suggest this strategy is worth considering. One drawback might be the difficulty of substantially scaling up from a program that has been project based.

If non–student aid efforts like provider reimbursement and TRIO were to substitute for loans in the payment of tuition and fees, the question remains how students would pay for their living expenses while enrolled in remedial programs. One option would be to allow the use of loans to pay for such expenses. Another would be to create a new stipend program for these students. A third option would be to allow Pell Grants to cover a standard amount of living expenses.

If using loans to finance instructional costs for remedial students is questionable, then using loans to pay for their living costs seems even more inappropriate. It seems more plausible and defensible that Pell Grants or some similar stipend be made available to cover the living costs of students while they participate in basic skills remediation programs.

■ Conference Discussion

Several speakers strongly opposed eliminating remedial students from Title IV eligibility. Student financial aid in the 1960s and 1970s, Dolores Cross argued, was meant to promote access to postsecondary education for "all eligible students." There was nothing in the legislation restricting aid to "students who were ready to do college-level work." In effect, Cross said, there was an "acknowledgment that many students would be underprepared and it was not a level playing field."

Some conferees also questioned whether there was an operationally useful definition of the term "college-ready student." Humphrey Doerman said in his experience, "college-level work is what the faculty says it is, and that varies from college to college and from department to department."[7]

Sandy Baum, an economist at Skidmore College, took a different tack when she observed, "Much of the increased participation over the past two decades has involved a redefinition of higher education, so that anyone getting any form of training after high school is counted in the college numbers. Raising these numbers should not necessarily be a policy goal."

Regardless of what is defined as "college," many conferees agreed that the growing reliance of remedial, at-risk students on loan financing is indeed worrisome. At Chicago State University, Cross said the "reality is many students are borrowing when they take remedial or developmental courses," and she is "the last person to be comfortable with the loan-grant imbalance" in financing the costs of these students.

Cross went on to emphasize the critical importance of academic support services for such students. Loan financing for students can only be justified if there is a program in place to facilitate their retention and graduation. "I think we have a moral responsibility," she said, "to set up a process whereby, if we admit these students who have been underserved, and if we don't want them to have a high level of debt, we help them succeed. And that's what we have done" at Chicago State. Cross reported that her institution now retains 66 percent of entering students through two years, as compared to 55 percent in 1989. It also has raised the graduation rate of students within six years of entering from 17 percent in 1989 to 23 per cent in 1994.

Institutions, Cross suggested, "need incentives for continuous progress in retaining and graduating students." In Illinois one reason such incentives are particularly urgent for public institutions is that the state says if a student with a deficiency is admitted, the school has the responsibility of either removing that deficiency or not accepting the student. Cross warned that such rules give schools a reason not to accept such students, which could ultimately narrow the reach of public higher education.

A number of other speakers underscored the importance of retention and completion for at-risk groups. Many said that the system's greatest disappointment is its failure to get more low-income students to complete college; student aid has worked beautifully for middle-class students, but not those from disadvantaged backgrounds.

A "passive educational system [that says to students] 'come if you want, take the course if you want'" does not work for today's high-risk students, Stephen Blair said. "Just putting money on the table" in the form of student aid is not the answer. Institutions must offer "a supportive structure, making sure students get the best diagnostics, the remediation, having somebody in their face if they start missing school," said Blair. Such students need "a commitment between the institution and the individual, that 'we together will help you succeed.' That's what makes the difference."

Elaine El-Khawas of the American Council on Education suggested it would be appropriate to have "effective academic support services" as a condition of institutional eligibility for Title IV funds. The higher education community has learned a great deal over the past ten or twenty years about serving underprepared students, she said. "Comprehensive academic support at the right time really works. Have we done it well? We have been half-hearted and incomplete about it; but some institutions (including big, famous universities) have learned that it really does work." A new criterion of the student aid system that focuses on academic support services could "reward the behaviors we want in institutions of all kinds," El-Khawas noted.

Cross urged that federal funds be provided to degree-granting institutions, both public and private, that have demonstrated they can improve the performance of at-risk students. The approach would be aimed at strengthening the capacity of these institutions to help at the precollege level, during college, and even perhaps after graduation by providing opportunities for their alumni to advance in careers or graduate studies. The funding of institutions, she suggested, could be based on a combination of need and the level of improvement relative to the student population.

Two programs under the Higher Education Act were suggested as possible vehicles to fund such institutional incentives for student support. Cross proposed redefining the State Student Incentives Grants (SSIG) program for this purpose. Institutions would qualify if they met performance criteria for serving students who were not college ready.

Lois Rice of the Brookings Institution suggested Title III of the HEA as another possible vehicle for encouraging institutions to help at-risk students. Originally intended for historically black colleges and universities (HBCUs) and now somewhat broader, Title III could provide incentives for institutions to support students who are not college ready. Rice, a strong advocate of student aid over institutional aid in the 1970s, suggested it may be time to revisit this old debate. Perhaps, she said, we need to "reward those degree-granting institutions that are truly making the effort to graduate these kids whom we are so concerned about."

THE SCOPE OF FEDERAL INVOLVEMENT

SHOULD THE FEDERAL GOVERNMENT PLAY A LARGER ROLE IN FOSTERING OR ESTABLISHING INSTITUTIONAL PERFORMANCE AND COST STANDARDS FOR POSTSECONDARY EDUCATION AND TRAINING?

The Goals 2000 legislation passed in 1994 formalizes an unprecedented national process for developing and certifying standards and assessments in elementary and secondary education. Will similar federal involvement eventually extend to postsecondary education as well? The diversity of American higher education, the diffuse nature of knowledge and learning at the postsecondary level, and American traditions of academic freedom and institutional autonomy all militate against such federal involvement. Nonetheless, it seems unlikely that the national standards debate will totally bypass postsecondary education.

If nothing else, the "access to what" question is unavoidable in developing future federal student aid policies. Policymakers and the public need to know whether the federal aid system provides access to postsecondary opportunities that meet standards of quality and provide an adequate return on the government's and the student's investments.

It also seems unlikely that the federal government will be willing to sit out the national debate on college affordability. Steep increases in tuition and other charges over the past decade and a half, and the inability of federal aid to keep pace with these escalating costs, represent an invitation to discuss what role the federal government might play in making college more affordable in the future.

How can the federal government reduce fraud and abuse in student aid programs and promote better institutional performance without overburdening well-performing institutions with regulation?

At least two kinds of improved institutional quality control can be contemplated. One involves steps the federal government can take to ensure that institutions provide programs of adequate quality to justify the expenditure of federal funds. Such an effort has and no doubt will continue to provoke considerable controversy as colleges and universities resist intrusions into academic life. Another approach to quality control is reduction of fraud and waste in the provision of federal aid funds.

Improving Federal Institutional Quality Control Efforts

Past efforts to ensure the quality of institutions participating in federal aid programs have not been very successful. The traditional method for ensuring institutional quality has been the so-called triad arrangement, in which private accreditation, state licensure, and federal eligibility provisions each played a part in assuring that students are attending institutions of adequate quality.

But each leg of the triad has failed in various ways and for different reasons. The accrediting bodies seem disinclined to discipline fee-paying member institutions and are ill equipped to do much of what they are being asked, particularly financial audits and assessments. The process by which state agencies license institutions is extremely fragmented; a state may have as many as a half-dozen different agencies responsible for licensing different types of institutions, with no overall interagency coordination. The federal process for approval of institutions and accrediting agencies is usually pro forma.

The most obvious indictment of the traditional triad arrangement is the increase over time in student loan default rates and federal costs. In response, in the late 1980s the federal government instituted default rate cutoffs as an additional means to weed out institutions that were not offering programs of minimal quality. Any institution with a default rate above a certain level for three consecutive years would be slated to lose eligibility to participate in federal student aid programs.

These cutoff procedures have been successful in terminating eligibility for a number of institutions. After several years of operation, default rates and federal costs have started to decline, although they remain unacceptably high. But the law still gives the benefit of the doubt to the institution and places the burden of proof on the government, which must demonstrate noncompliance. This limits the effectiveness of the process, as institutions that are clearly problematic are able to continue operating for years.

Default rate cutoffs also tend to be imprecise policy tools that do nothing about institutions with very high rates of default that are nonetheless below the cutoff level. As a result, they encourage activities that bring an institution's rate just below the cutoff, such as an institution buying up a few bad loans or postponing a default long enough that it is not factored into the default rate. In addition, most defaults occur at institutions with default rates below the cutoff level. Thus, the cutoff procedure has become more a treatment of symptoms rather than a real solution.

Recognition that the triad has been ineffective and that the cutoff procedure was having limited success led to an extended discussion during the 1992 reauthorization about what other steps the federal government could take. The solution provided in the legislation is to give greater authority to new state agencies to review the credentials of institutions identified as being in trouble. These new legislative provisions and the regulations implementing them have the potential to improve the federal government's quality control capability. But many of the new state agencies are no better prepared to take on this responsibility than those agencies that were asked to do the job in the past.

In addition, the 1992 legislation does a poor job of delegating within the triad by asking all parties to do all things. The resulting redundancy of functions is both inefficient and confusing and will surely require future legislative and regulatory refinements.

Several means of improving the federal government's institutional quality control capabilities should be considered. One would be to rely more on performance measures as a means for judging institutional quality. The student-right-to-know legislation enacted several years ago requires institutions to develop and provide outcome measures (such as completion and placement rates) but does not integrate this information into the student aid eligibility process. Such an integration could contribute to better quality control in federal aid programs.

Some argue it would be better to focus more on an institution's federal program record than on its academic performance as a gauge of institutional quality, at least for purposes of federal student aid eligibility. Federal program performance measures (such as default rates, audit reviews, and the retention rates of aid recipients) would seem more within the federal government's ability to collect and less objectionable than academic performance measures (such as graduation rates), which are difficult to collect on a systematic basis. Moreover, since the question is whether institutions are using federal funds appropriately, federal program performance seems the more relevant measure.

Regardless of which type of performance measure is used, this shift would permit the kind of regulatory relief and reform many colleges and universities are requesting. The sheer magnitude and complexity of the regulations institutions must now comply with to qualify for federal aid has led to widespread calls for regulatory relief. But good policy dictates that such relief be accompanied by some alternative quality control mechanism. Greater reliance on performance measures might be part of the answer.

Another vehicle for regulatory relief would be to introduce financial incentives and penalties in lieu of federal regulations and rules. For example, institutions might be charged a fee based on the number of their students who default. As mentioned earlier, the default rate cutoff procedures tend to encourage institutions to get below the cutoff line, but they do nothing to prevent the bulk of defaults that occur at institutions with default rates below the cutoff. Risk-sharing for lenders was introduced in the 1993 student loan reform legislation, and it might be worth considering for institutions as well.

Reducing Fraud, Waste, and Abuse in Federal Student Aid

No discussion of improving quality and standards would be complete without addressing the need to reduce fraud, waste, and abuse. This is an elemental form of quality control. Taxpayers have every right to expect that the federal government will take steps to save money through the systematic elimination of fraud, waste, and abuse.

But because a wide spectrum of activity can reasonably fall into the category of fraud, waste, and abuse, policy discussions on the potential for such savings need to be clear about what is being considered. This spectrum stretches from pure criminality (such as falsification of records) to mismanagement (for example, failure to recognize that a program does not qualify for federal aid) to policy decisions that are "wasteful" (such as expanding eligibility for middle-class students who do not need such aid to go to college).

How much potential savings are there in these broad categories? The honest answer is that an estimate is difficult to make; it depends in part on which kind of waste is being discussed. The savings from eliminating outright criminality would probably be fairly low—perhaps less than 5 percent of all student aid expenditures. Mismanagement probably adds another 5 percent to the total.

However, a much larger percentage of federal aid dollars would be under discussion to the extent policies currently in effect are reexamined. For example, many student aid recipients do not complete their course of study, which is also the case for all college students. Although there is nothing inherently fraudulent or abusive in students trying and failing, it would nonetheless be appropriate for federal policymakers to focus on ways to improve the completion or graduation rate of aid recipients as a means of improving federal program performance.

■ Conference Discussion

Jane Wellman of the Institute for Higher Education Policy led off the discussion with a thorough critique of the current accountability model under Title IV of the Higher Education Act, which she said is not working well. The result has been "a glob of regulations that are internally conflicted, impossible to understand, and difficult to communicate to institutions. Institutions don't know what they are supposed to do; and because the regulations are so far beyond the enforcement capacity of the federal government, they are unevenly enforced."

State postsecondary review entities (SPREs) will create a massive review and oversight process, Wellman predicted, but when all is said and done, under the rules state decisionmakers will be unwilling or unable to get low-performing institutions out of Title IV. Meanwhile the accreditation process has been "essentially federalized and made into a regulatory extension of the Department of Education. . . . Accreditation has many problems, but the solution is not to make it more regulatory."

Wellman concluded that "we need different vehicles for getting at fraud and abuse and for getting at quality. I also don't think we need to do everything through Title IV." She said the federal government could attempt to set goals and performance measures for higher education, but it would be "more constructive to frame the discussion in that context, rather than in Title IV regulatory terms. . . . We are trying to shoehorn way too much into a regulatory model."

David Longanecker, assistant secretary of education, responded by noting that the federal government's dilemma is that its job is not to monitor academic performance, yet it does have to set minimum standards to assure that federal funds are properly accounted for. An undesirable result is that, for many institutions, these minimal conditions become maximum expectations. Further, the minimums send other institutions "a message of relatively low expectations."

Longanecker disagreed that SPREs are a failure; with no SPRE operating yet, he pointed out, it is too soon to judge. But he did agree that the Department of Education's regulations need to be fashioned better; they are often excessive and redundant, based on a history of lack of trust among members of the triad. He further agreed that all of the department's energies should not be consumed with Title IV accountability. He said it is important to "draw the distinction between our role in running federal programs and our role in fostering a national dialogue" on standards and expectations for higher education.

Longanecker also reminded the audience that it was Congress that came up with "a very tightfisted, regulatory model" in the 1992 law. "I would have drafted it differently," he said, but what Congress enacted is what the department has had to implement. He further cautioned that these legislative provisions were passed not just out of congressional concern about fiscal fraud and abuse. They also emanated from broader public and congressional "disaffection with the higher education community writ large." Until such broader concerns are addressed, Longanecker warned, the sector may face continued regulatory pressure.

Several conferees suggested that issuance of postsecondary standards should be viewed in the context of the broader debate on national goals for education. Clifford Adelman of the Department of Education reminded the group that the goals established following the Education Summit of 1989 included ones for higher education, but "in Goals 2000, higher education doesn't exist. We lost all the pieces, and when we lose the pieces we get marginalized and get into battles over regulations." This is happening, Adelman said, because "higher education is not part of the national vision of improving quality, degree completion, and other social objectives." Jane Wellman agreed. "It would be very helpful to have a conversation about national goals in higher education. We haven't had it yet," she said.

James Mingle pointed out that the discussion of standards for postsecondary education also needs to be viewed in the context of changing taxpayer expectations at both the state and federal levels. "If we were having this conversation twenty or thirty years ago," Mingle said, "it would have been about enrollment—what kind of access are we providing?—and about resources—how much money are we getting over last year? But now, in state capitals and lately at the federal level, we are having a different conversation. It is about student success and how we might judge whether we're getting a return on our investment."

Many speakers supported making a sharper distinction between rules for fiscal accountability on the one hand and broader quality assurance on the other. There was also clear support for eliminating redundancies in the allocation of functions within the triad. Both the legislation and the regulations, it was generally agreed, ultimately need to be streamlined and rationalized.

Walter Moulton, director of financial aid at Bowdoin College, wished the rules would distinguish between institutions that are above suspicion of fraud and abuse and the borderline institutions where thorough accounting and heavy paperwork are appropriately required. "If an institution is doing very, very well after years of audits, and there is no signal at all we are guilty of fraud and abuse, why are we held to the same standards as everyone else? There's no benefit for the institution that's doing a very good job." James Mingle said in response that with some refinement the new process should eventually work the way Moulton advocated. The SPRE agencies are supposed to screen out the fine performers and relieve them of extra reporting through a series of screens and "triggers." One conference participant suggested a rating system like that for bonds to more clearly distinguish those whose accountability should not be in question.

Mingle said the states are trying to implement accountability in a responsible way. Either through their own legislation or through SPRE, the states are looking at multiple measures, not a lone one. States are also applying different measures and giving them varying weight depending on the goals of the individual institution being reviewed.

Longanecker raised fundamental questions about "whether the way we do accreditation in this country is a modern quality assurance process—whether it makes any sense to send three people out to a campus for four days." He spoke of "getting to a different world" in the monitoring of postsecondary institutions.

David Pierce, president of the American Association of Community Colleges, said accreditation is currently going through a self-analysis. Pierce suggested that institutions and accrediting agencies need to "build a culture of responsibility" that is positive and activist rather than reactive. He then urged the Department of Education to join in the search for nonregulatory solutions.

Mingle said the accrediting world is struggling with how to move away from "faculty-driven resource standards to standards that indicate whether learning is taking place." For this conversion to occur, however, incentives will need to be adjusted so that it is more clearly in the institutions' self-interest to do a good academic job with students. For example, institutions that are in trouble should welcome measures to demonstrate they are improving. Such a new culture of accreditation could be developed under present rules, said Longanecker, but he and others at the conference agreed it will take major adjustments to bring this about.

More modern ways to report on institutions could include the "thick description" used by some social scientists, suggested Ernst Benjamin of the American Association of University Professors. For example, perhaps the whole accreditation report on an institution, rather than a summary, should be published. Complex quantitative indicators can be tried, but these have the drawback of usually being unintelligible to laymen (that is, most public policymakers). Charles Clotfelter, economics professor and vice provost at Duke University, said it is instructive to look at the "scorecards" being devised by states for K-12 schools. In his experience, multiple regression analysis in these exercises tends to be understood only by consultants, and it is quickly supplanted by other measurement methods that policymakers can understand.

Ron Ehrenberg, an economist at Cornell University, said arguments about the diversity and complexity of higher education should not be an excuse for saying "we can't measure it." Why does higher education not provide "basic information such as graduation rates and what students did afterward?" Hospitals face much the same problem with patient census information, yet they do it. Likewise, law and other professional school associations offer public directories that show student GPAs, graduation statistics, and postgraduation employment data. "It would be more complex for an entire university, but we owe it to consumers to provide such information," Ehrenberg said.

David Longanecker summarized the discussion by noting that a fully modern quality control process would include, besides public reports, mechanisms to encourage, measure, and publicize continuous improvement and timeliness of updating. He noted that while the traditional triad figures out how to do all this, *Money* magazine, *U.S. News and World Report*, and other media outlets are giving consumers the data they seek about schools.

What rules or incentives might the federal government consider to encourage institutions to moderate the growth in tuition and the underlying costs of educating students, thereby making college more affordable?

Much has been written and said over the past decade about making college more affordable. The tuition spiral has led millions of parents and their children to wonder and worry whether they will be able to afford a college education.

A number of important books and reports on higher education finance in recent years have echoed the theme of affordability. In 1991 the Brookings Institution published a book by Michael McPherson and Morton Schapiro, *Keeping College Affordable*.[8] In 1993 the congressionally chartered National Commission on Responsibilities for Financing Postsecondary Education received widespread publicity over its report, *Making College Affordable Again*.[9]

These and other reports have focused primarily on how to increase the aid available for the rising tuitions and other charges that have captured so much public attention and concern. What has been missing in many of these discussions, however, is the other side of the affordability equation—namely, how to reduce the growth in the cost of a college education. Ultimately, making college affordable again will depend at least as much on reducing the rate of increase in tuitions and other charges as on providing more aid.

This task of reducing the rate of price increases should be the responsibility of each of the groups now involved in financing higher education: the federal government, state governments, employers, and colleges and universities, as well as students and their families.

Because federal funds represent only about one-tenth of all revenue sources for American higher education, it would probably not be realistic or appropriate for the federal government to try to influence institutional pricing policies directly. Yet through the need-based aid system, federal policies do have a relationship to the tuition, fees, and other charges set by institutions. Eligibility under most federal programs is determined by a student's need, defined as the difference between the cost of attendance and what the student's family can reasonably be expected to contribute. (The Pell Grant Program is the principal exception to this need-based approach, as cost of attendance plays a small to nonexistent role in determining the size of the award.)

An implicit assumption of federal need-based aid is that the very provision of aid will not influence how much an institution charges. Nonetheless, there has been a nagging concern raised by analysts and policymakers over the years that aid policies may indeed create incentives for institutions to price according to the availability of federal dollars. Under the need-based equation, after all, whenever an institution increases its charges, it may (depending on program limits and availability of funds) increase the eligibility of its students for federal assistance.

As we have noted earlier, the evidence suggests that this concern is most relevant for the proprietary (for-profit) sector of postsecondary education. Most schools in this sector rely on federal student aid for at least half of their total revenues. Many could not exist without federal student aid, and some set their fees to maximize revenues from such aid. It seems reasonable that federal policies should recognize this reality and do something about it.

For nonprofit institutions, the concern that aid availability might affect tuitions and other charges has been less worrisome because most colleges and universities are not nearly as dependent on federal funds as trade schools. Because many or most of the students at these nonprofit institutions do not receive federal aid, the impact of price hikes on their students is not necessarily cushioned by federal support.

Moreover, federal limits on how much students could borrow in the past have been set low enough so that when private colleges (and higher-priced public institutions) increased their charges, the eligibility to borrow of most students was unaffected because they were already borrowing the maximum amount. But increases in federal loan limits in the 1992 reauthorization—especially the extension of unsubsidized student loans to all undergraduates and the decision to allow parents to borrow up to the full costs of attendance—represent an avenue by which student loans could fuel higher tuitions in the future at nonprofit institutions as well as for-profit trade schools.

One conceivable approach to ensure that federal policies do not encourage higher tuitions would be to limit aid provided to students attending institutions where tuitions and fees have increased more rapidly than some standard set by the government. While he was U.S. Secretary of Education, William Bennett suggested that federal aid be limited for students at institutions where tuition and fees increased faster than the inflation rate plus 1 percent.

The main difficulty with linking aid eligibility to growth in what institutions charge is that tuition, fees, and other charges can be manipulated without any real change in policy. For example, certain costs now included in tuition could instead be charged as user fees on a student-by-student basis. Another argument against such an approach is that the easiest way for most institutions to lower their charges is to reduce the amount of aid they provide—a policy direction that most observers consider detrimental to the goal of greater access to higher education.

Another way to apply cost containment to postsecondary education would be for the federal government to establish reasonable cost standards for use in federal student aid programs. How might these reasonable cost standards work? The U.S. secretary of education could issue an annual schedule of reasonable costs for different types of postsecondary education and training. The secretary might publish one standard for four-year academic undergraduate education, one for two-year academic programs, and then a variety for different kinds of vocational training. These standards would be related to how much it reasonably costs to provide training in automobile mechanics, cosmetology, computer programming, and so on. In addition, through the cost standards the secretary could establish a reasonable level of nontuition expenses that the federal government would reimburse as well. This kind of cost standard for nontuition expenses already exists for Pell Grants and could easily be transferred to other aid programs.

In some respects, the reasonable cost standards described here would be similar to the use of diagnostic review groups (DRGs) in health care, in that they would establish what the federal government would be willing to pay for an enumerated set of services. One difference is that services in higher education would be bunched together in a few categories, whereas there are literally hundreds of DRG items in health care.

In another important respect, reasonable cost standards in higher education would be very different from the DRG health care model: Colleges and universities would be under no obligation to charge what the secretary of education deemed a reasonable cost standard. Instead, cost standards would be used solely to determine a student's eligibility for federal aid.

A principal argument against this approach is that it could put students at risk, because the federal government would no longer fully meet documented need. But this ignores the fact that few students now receive all their aid from the federal government. For most students, the last dollar of aid comes from their institutions. The primary impact of imposing reasonable federal cost standards would most likely be that institutions would either: (1) provide more aid to their students to meet the difference between the federal cost standards and what they actually charge; or (2) adjust their tuition to recognize the limits imposed by these standards.

■ Conference Discussion

David Longanecker made it clear that the Clinton administration does not see tuition growth and cost containment as a federal responsibility. It is the responsibility of the states to address cost issues at state institutions and the responsibility of trustees to do so at private institutions.

He added that college tuitions are already so far beyond any level the government could fund that "we have had to take a fatalistic perspective on tuition increases. There is no way we can possibly keep up. . . . So we look to other areas to make a difference. We might provide incentives for those institutions that show some restraint. . . . But we would not be comfortable establishing the right price."

At the same time, Longanecker said, the Department of Education wants to ensure that its programs do not give institutions an incentive to raise tuitions even further than they otherwise would. "We don't want federal programs to exacerbate the problem—to have prices increase for all students because of policies we might implement affecting some students."

Charles Clotfelter challenged the common perception that federal student aid policies were a primary cause of private-sector tuition growth in the 1980s. In a study he conducted at four private institutions, he found that tuitions went up for "reasons that were unique to the decade." During the 1980s the national income distribution shifted, making wealthy Americans wealthier. The costs of professional salaries also went up dramatically, meaning institutions needed to pay faculty more; and there was a "surge in demand resulting from a jump in the economic rate of return on a college education." Several other conditions also facilitated tuition growth. Inflation was so low that the increased income from big tuition increases was mostly real. Also, when these institutions looked at their competitors who were doing the same thing, they found there was safety in numbers. Finally, the financial aid environment provided a safety net for the neediest students, as all of these institutions subscribed to a covenant that they would base their financial aid to students on need.

Clotfelter observed that since the conditions of the 1980s are unlikely to be repeated in the next several years, he believes growth in private college tuition will moderate. He further reported that his study showed that federal aid dollars funded only 5 percent of the increase in tuition growth at these private institutions; the rest was funded by the institutions themselves, through tuition, philanthropy, and other nonfederal sources. Thus, federal aid did not seem to be a major factor in explaining the growth in private college tuition.

Sandy Baum suggested that a slowing of tuition growth in the private sector might have a negative effect on student choice, because there would be less tuition revenue at private institutions to fund financial aid budgets.

Clotfelter said people used to talk about twin public policy objectives in financial aid: access and choice. Choice was the probability that a poor young man or woman could go to Harvard, or one of perhaps fifty other institutions that provide special avenues to leadership and socioeconomic status in American society. "Who is financing that policy today? It's the institutions," Clotfelter noted. "We have to worry, though, when these institutions start bailing out of the need-blind full financing—the old need-based aid covenant. When that unravels, this thing called choice will go downhill."

A number of conferees shared Clotfelter's concern about the extent to which private institutions already appear to be backing off the need-blind policies of the 1980s. Some conferees asked whether the federal government could respond in some way to reverse this trend away from need-based standards. The flip side of this question was also raised: whether federal aid policy should be driven by the fifty or so institutions that still are able to afford need-blind admissions policies and to meet potential students' full need.

Other conferees were equally or even more concerned with trends in public sector pricing and financial aid. Ron Ehrenberg disagreed with the notion that the "only road to success is through the elite [private] universities." The federal and state obligation, Ehrenberg argued, is to "provide choice, so that at least people can attend the top public institutions in each state, and we're not doing that now." Ehrenberg called for high-tuition and high-aid policies in the states—raising tuition levels in the flagship state institutions and plowing the money back into substantial grant aid for needy students. Well-off students, he said, should understand that they are still being subsidized, because their tuition does not cover the full costs of their education. Nor do their parents' taxes cover these costs, because many people in the state are paying taxes who do not have children attending college.

Leonard Wenc, director of financial aid at Carleton College, expressed a similar view in advocating a "more rational distribution of tax dollars" in the states. To the extent states keep tuitions relatively low in the public sector, "middle- and upper-middle-class families get the best deal. They don't even have to fill out the forms! All they have to do is show up at the bursar's office and fork over a discounted amount of dollars . . . to go the flagship state institution."

Demographic factors may actually moderate public tuition growth in some states, observed Thomas Kane of the Brookings Institution. He said public tuitions rose in the past because enrollments were growing and the states came under pressure to limit outlays, since they carry most of public higher education's cost. The states let more of the cost be borne by tuition payers, and tuitions went up. Thus in states where the college-bound population will level off or decline, there may not be as much pressure toward tuition increases. On the other hand, in most southern and western states where the number of students attending college are predicted to increase significantly, tuitions may have to rise to pay the cost of new enrollments. Others suggested, to the contrary, that states with growing enrollments will be better positioned to moderate their charges because they will be able to spread their fixed costs over a larger number of students.

STRENGTHENING CURRENT PROGRAMS

HOW COULD THE EXISTING STUDENT AID PROGRAMS BE MODIFIED TO INCREASE THEIR EFFECTIVENESS IN RAISING COLLEGE PARTICIPATION RATES AMONG TARGETED GROUPS OF STUDENTS?

The preceding two sections have examined broad issues in the design and regulation of the federal student aid system and how federal policy might better achieve the goal of access to a quality education at reasonable cost. The following section examines a further series of possible changes in the student aid structure aimed at making existing programs more effective in meeting various federal policy goals.

Would consolidating the current array of federal aid programs reduce complexity and make the system more understandable to students and families?

The number of federal student aid programs has multiplied since they were first enacted, and so has their complexity. The federal student aid system now includes a half-dozen grant programs, a dozen loan programs (as a result of the 1993 student loan reform legislation that created a direct loan program to mirror each of the guaranteed loan programs), as well as a college work-study program. This list excludes the many state and private efforts and dozens of federal fellowships and other aid programs for various groups of students.

The eligibility rules vary greatly. Many programs require separate applications; prospective recipients are often unaware of the federal aid programs and therefore may not realize they are eligible. In short, the complexity of the system gets in the way of the programs meeting their objectives.

A frequently mentioned proposal to streamline student aid has been to consolidate all of the existing programs into only three—one grant, one loan, and one work-study. This proposal has been advanced from time to time over the past decade as a way to make the federal aid system more understandable to students and their families.

One argument against this kind of program consolidation is that it might reduce the discretion the institutional financial aid office has in packaging aid for the individual student. On-campus aid officers are usually in the best position to judge the particular needs of students. The federal campus-based aid programs have been a principal source of discretionary funds allowing aid officers to make such judgments.

A variant on the consolidation proposal that addresses this concern about aid officer discretion would be to consolidate existing federal campus-based aid into one program that would allow aid officers to provide at least grants and work-study from a single federal allocation.

■ **Conference Discussion**

Opinion was divided on whether the number of federal programs truly represents a barrier to access by increasing the system's complexity from the point of view of students and their families, and whether the benefits of consolidation outweigh the advantage of having multiple programs tailored to meet the needs of different groups of students.

Martin Kramer, a consultant on higher education, said that in his opinion the main argument for consolidation would be the possibility of federal cost savings that might be used to increase funding for Pell Grants. But Kramer doubted that program consolidation is realistic or would make the student aid system much more intelligible. "Even if you consolidate federal programs," he pointed out, "you still have multiple state and institutional programs. Besides, a conceptual consolidation goes on now anyway." Most students and parents, he said, figure things out: how much they have to contribute, how much they will receive from the college, how much they have to earn, and how much to borrow.

Other speakers, on the contrary, thought consolidation might give both students and administrators a clearer picture of the two most important elements from the student point of view: grant aid and self-help in the form of loans and work-study. Walter Moulton said he would like to see just two programs, one grant and one self-help, "because it doesn't matter whether it's loans or work— either way, the burden lands on the students. Either they work now [during college] or they work later [to pay off the loans]. It's a timing question."

Moulton went on to argue that what is lacking in the aid system is an underlying yardstick that provides "the capacity to judge where self help should cut out and grant should cut in." So the system goes on "calmly overburdening" students with debt simply because they are eligible under the rules to borrow. This "create[s] default situations by lending people more than they can really repay with their earning power after graduation." He favored consolidations that offer administrators and students a better purchase on this issue.

Robert Huff of the Hoover Institute argued that consolidation would make student aid more vulnerable to budget cuts; each of the current programs has its proponents, and merging them would dilute that basis for defense.

André Bell, dean of enrollment at Bentley College, urged that any consolidation plan be based on clear policy about who the target of federal student aid is. Now, Bell noted, "[the] target is everyone," meaning there is something for all—the middle class, disadvantaged Americans, "all eligible students," and so on. Bell also urged targeting the form of education deemed most desirable: hitting the bull's-eye would be to get low-income students through four years to earn the baccalaureate degree. Many students would place in the outer rings, so to speak, in two-year colleges and trade schools. But at least the system would then have clear-sighted priorities and, if the focus remained on disadvantaged students, aid programs would be less coopted by the middle class.

Should an overall maximum be established on the amount of federal aid an individual student may receive?

There is no overall annual or cumulative limit on how much federal aid a student may receive. Instead, aid limits are set on a program-by-program basis. Students from low-income families typically are eligible for the full range of federal programs and can receive up to $15,000 or more in federal aid per year, although few receive this much. Students from middle-income families are eligible for modest amounts of grants and the full range of loan programs; upper-income undergraduate students can participate only through the parent loan (PLUS) and unsubsidized loan programs.

As a result, practically no one knows how much federal aid individual students are eligible to receive. In addition, the federal government provides little if any direction to institutions on how to package the aid they are allocated. Two students with identical financial circumstances attending the same institution may receive very different amounts and mixes of federal aid. This inconsistency in the level and mix of aid was one of the principal concerns that led to passage of the Basic Grants (now Pell Grants) legislation in 1972. Yet the problem persists today.

In 1993 the absence of overall aid limits and the lack of coherence in federal aid policies led the bipartisan National Commission on Responsibilities for Financing Postsecondary Education to suggest the establishment of a federal aid maximum. Under this proposal all full-time college students would be eligible for the same total amount of federal aid per year. However, the mix of grant, loan, and work aid that students could receive would vary according to their family financial circumstances, with the neediest students getting the most grant aid and wealthy students only eligible for unsubsidized loans.

Under the National Commission's recommendation, the total annual amount of federal aid a student could receive would be the lesser of the student's cost of attendance (tuition, fees, room, board, and other expenses) or the maximum amount of federal aid as specified in statute. A student's expected family contribution would be subtracted from the lesser of these two amounts; the result of that subtraction would determine the eligibility of that student for subsidized aid. Unsubsidized loans would be used to ensure that all students were eligible for the same uniform amount of federal aid.

The National Commission argued that instituting a federal aid maximum could simplify what has become an overly complex federal aid system. Students and their parents would be much more certain about their eligibility for federal aid.

In addition, the aid maximum might give policymakers a handle on the loan/grant imbalance by setting out a policy on what the mix of loans, grants, and work-study should be for different groups of students. This would be in sharp contrast to the current situation, wherein no policy exists and loans are allowed to grow without relation to the availability of grants.

Although the National Commission's report does not connect its suggestion for a federal aid maximum to the concept of cost containment, such a maximum does have the potential for a modest degree of cost containment. By severing the link between aid availability and tuitions and other costs of attendance at institutions charging more than the federal aid maximum, future increases in the costs of attendance above the aid maximum would play no role in determining eligibility for federal aid. In effect, a federal aid maximum would make the federal student loan programs income based (just as the Pell Grants program has been since its inception) rather than need based.

One effect of creating a federal aid maximum would probably be convergence between public and private tuitions. That is, on the margin, the aid maximum would help to slow the growth in private sector tuitions, because future tuition increases would not result in any additional federal aid. At the same time, a federal aid maximum theoretically would serve as an incentive for public colleges to increase their charges to maximize their students' aid eligibility, although this incentive to increase charges in the future would be no greater than it is today under a need-based system.

An immediate problem with the federal aid maximum as proposed by the National Commission was its price tag: $6 billion to $7 billion more than the federal government currently spends per year on student aid. Federal budget constraints clearly ruled this out. But virtually all of the federal spending increase called for in the National Commission's report was attributable to its recommendation to increase the Pell Grant maximum to the fully authorized level of $3,700. This increase in Pell Grants is not a necessary condition for putting a federal aid maximum in place. The net federal cost of instituting a federal aid maximum per se is zero or even negative, assuming no change in the policies governing individual aid programs.

If the concept of a federal aid maximum is worthy of further consideration, then a number of other decisions must be made in developing a legislative proposal.

—How much should the federal aid maximum be, and how should it grow over time?

—Should the maximum vary for different types of students—in particular, should a distinction be made between the amount of aid available to undergraduates and graduate students?

—Should the maximum aid amount apply to all federal student aid programs, or only to certain programs?

■ Conference Discussion

Sandy Baum called the aid maximum a "false simplification" that glosses over the problems of financial aid rather than solving them. "What it says is that financial aid consists of grants, work, subsidized loans, and unsubsidized loans, and we advertise that everyone can have aid. But then some are going to find out it's all in unsubsidized loans. That's misleading, once again playing into the idea that the target is everyone." Moreover, she noted, a cap on aid says to a student who wants to go to an expensive school, "'we're not going to provide as much liquidity as you need,'" thus hindering the goal of choice. The aid maximum, she argued, "doesn't get us away from the hard decisions" about the make-up of the package, the loan-grant balance, the need for liquidity, and the need for subsidies.

Bell argued that the aid maximum "doesn't address the primary question of access for the neediest population. How does it motivate people who are averse to borrowing to buy in?"

Maureen McLaughlin was more positive about the potential of a guaranteed aid maximum to move the system in the direction of predictability. It "would tell students early, while they are in high school and making academic decisions, what they will be eligible for."

Although there was no consensus on the aid maximum concept, there was general agreement on the importance of early awareness of aid as well as better understanding of the aid process among students and families. "When you ask people about aid, they are confused about what they can get, how much, how to apply, how to fill out the forms. The confusion runs the gamut," McLaughlin added. Middle-class families tend to be better informed and more aggressive in using the system, but many speakers thought lower-income families often do not know how much help is there or how to go about obtaining it.

Thomas Kane noted that this could explain why there is not much clear evidence that Pell Grants have increased the proportion of low-income enrollments in the past. "I called Bunker Hill Community College in Boston last year and told them I was a researcher, but they misunderstood me. After I made a good faith effort to explain what I was doing, they nonetheless sent me the financial aid application forms. I've got a lot of education under my belt, but when I looked at these forms, it was not a trivial thing to fill them out. They scare me as much as my tax forms, and I pay somebody to help me with my taxes." The extent to which the application process remains difficult to understand or intimidating to potential aid recipients may go far toward explaining why federal policies have not been more successful in raising the participation rates of disadvantaged groups.

Mary Lee Hoganson, a secondary school counselor from Chicago, spoke about the "intimidation of the system" and the "kids that never make it into the system." She said guidance counselors need training in financial aid so they have a more sophisticated understanding of the process and can more effectively steer students and families through it. Many counselors "know more about the NCAA eligibility rules than about the federal methodology for computing aid," Hoganson noted. "The information isn't getting out, and counselors are telling kids they can't qualify for aid when they do."

Although there was little support for a guaranteed federal aid maximum to address these problems, several ideas were suggested that might help achieve some of the same objectives. For example, the idea returned to most often in all three conference sessions was that a much more significant portion of federal student aid should take the form of grants rather than loans in at least the first year of study. This, it was argued, could increase access and retention while lowering defaults in the system as a whole.

Half of those who drop out of school, it was pointed out, do so in the first year, so that is the point of greatest risk. Grants should therefore be "frontloaded" when the student is starting out in college, with loans "backloaded" for those who persist beyond the first two undergraduate years. One advantage of frontloading, proponents argued, would be that if students discovered college was not for them, they would not be saddled with loan repayments. This might reduce defaults, since those who leave after one year or less default at a higher rate than those who stay in college longer.

Also, because frontloading would direct grants toward more marginal students—those in their first years—it could provide institutions with an incentive to serve higher-risk students. It is possible that frontloading grant aid might not decrease defaults, only shift them to occur later. But students who complete college are better prepared for higher-skilled, better-paying jobs, and they are therefore more able to repay loans than those who enter the job market after only a year or two of college. So frontloading seems to have a chance of lowering defaults overall.

Ken Regner of the National Institute of Independent Colleges and Universities expressed concern that frontloading of grants might create a disincentive for students to complete their baccalaureate degrees. David Breneman, professor of education at Harvard University, agreed that there is a bait-and-switch aspect to the frontloading strategy. However, he argued that "those who complete and see their first two years as a success are in a far better position to be borrowers than those just starting out. . . . I worry a lot more about the ones who don't get started."

Ron Ehrenberg suggested a variation on frontloading: "We should load grants in the first year, to encourage people to experiment with college. After the first year, they will have a sense if they are going to succeed, so the second year is the time for loans. It would be a boon for the two-year colleges to load all the money in the first two years. But that would be a mistake because then two-year college students would have less incentive to go on to four-year institutions. So we should think of a mix of years—odd-numbered years heavy in grants, even-numbered years heavy in loans."

What changes in Pell Grant eligibility and award rules should be considered to permit higher maximum awards within currently projected budgets?

In twenty years, Pell Grants have grown from a fledgling program unable to fully spend an initial $50 million appropriation on just full-time freshmen to one that strained against its $6 billion annual appropriation in the early 1990s three years running. During this period, Pell Grants became a principal form of federal student aid, surpassing the combined assistance available through the GI Bill, social security benefits for college students, and Supplemental Educational Opportunity Grants, all programs that preceded the existence of Pell Grants.

However, in recent years it has become clear that without modification, Pell Grants are unlikely to achieve the goal of increasing the college participation and completion rates of economically disadvantaged college students. Under current program eligibility and award rules, it has become extremely difficult to raise the maximum award. Because of the accumulated effects of legislative expansion, it now requires $400 million or more to raise the Pell Grant maximum award by just $100 for all students; this is in contrast to only several years ago, when less than $200 million was required to increase the maximum award by $100.

Thus, while the Pell Grant maximum is currently authorized at $3,900 (academic year 1994–95), the actual maximum award has stagnated at $2,300 in recent years, its value nearly 50 percent lower in real dollars than it was a decade ago. Figure 8 shows the rapidly declining share of the cost of attendance covered by Pell Grants at both public and private four-year institutions.

Moreover, the Pell Grants program has been in the spotlight as a result of congressional hearings, which highlighted questionable or

FIGURE 8. *Maximum Pell Grant as a Share of Cost of Attendance, 1973–93*

Percent

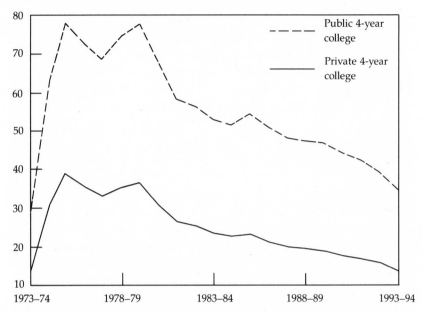

Source: Thomas Mortenson, "Purchasing Power of the Pell Grant Maximum 1973–74 to 1993–94," *Postsecondary Education OPPORTUNITY*, vol. 12 (April 1993), p. 10.

fraudulent practices in the program's administration that clearly require review and reform. These include the number of years for which some individuals receive Pell Grants and instances in which ineligible or nonexistent students qualified as Pell Grant recipients. Such abuses clearly require program reforms, which might free up funds to help raise the maximum award.

Altering Program Eligibility

Although Pell Grants were initially conceived as a program to help the most economically disadvantaged students pay for college, eligibility over time has been expanded, largely to enhance the continued political viability of the program. Periodically, the rules for what families are expected to contribute have been relaxed, including contributions from income and how much of parental assets (particularly equity in a home or farm) is available to meet the costs of a college education. But decisions to expand eligibility to maintain political viability may dilute the program's effectiveness in helping those students who are truly economically disadvantaged go to college.

Retargeting Pell Grant eligibility on the basis of family income, however, would not result in a large increase in the maximum award. Legislated reductions in what families are expected to contribute have not led to the significant increase in middle-class recipients that Congress anticipated. Most middle-income students remain ineligible for Pell Grants under the new rules, because their family contributions still exceed the maximum award.[10] Thus, restricting Pell Grant eligibility to students with family income less than $30,000, for example, would result in at most a $50 to $100 increase in the maximum award for those students who remain eligible for Pell Grants.

Students who are financially independent of their parents are another group for whom the issue of targeting is relevant. In the past several reauthorizations, the eligibility of independent students who are married or have children has been substantially expanded by the requirement that the income and assets of these students be treated the same as that of the parents of financially dependent students. At the same time, the 1992 legislation sharply restricted the eligibility of single independent students, with the result that 500,000 to 1 million Pell Grant recipients had their awards reduced substantially or eliminated altogether.

In effect, the tightened eligibility of single independent students paid for the increased eligibility of other groups of independent students and the expanded eligibility for dependent students, as well as the higher loan limits in the 1992 law. Redressing the effects of this change by restoring some or all of the eligibility of single independent students would make it even more difficult to increase the Pell Grant maximum award.

The retargeting of Pell Grants that would net the most federal savings would be to eliminate Pell Grant eligibility for remedial students or for those in short-term vocational training. But this kind of retargeting once again raises issues about what alternative financing mechanism might be used for these students.

Revising the Pell Award Formula

In the discussions leading up to the 1992 reauthorization of the Higher Education Act, higher education associations proposed a revision in the Pell Grant award formula that would have made it more sensitive to differences in tuitions, at least at a broad range of public institutions. This proposal was included in the House version of the bill. However, it was so watered down in the final conference agreement that in the current legislation there is no sensitivity to tuition and other cost differentials within foreseeable levels of funding.

Traditionally, the Pell Grant program has not been sensitive to tuition and cost-of-living differentials except by limiting awards to a percentage of costs of attendance and assuming a lower cost of living for students living at home than those living elsewhere. These restrictive provisions particularly affected community college students living at home who had little or no expectation of family contribution.

To address these concerns, the 1992 legislation eliminated the cost of attendance limitation and provided that students living at home be eligible for the same amount of aid as students living on or off campus. This increased the amount of each Pell Grant award available to students living at home by several hundred dollars. But while addressing certain inequities in the program, this change also substantially increased the level of funds needed to pay for any given level of the maximum award, thus adding to the difficulty of Pell Grants keeping up with increases in tuitions and other costs of attendance.

One means for increasing the maximum award within foreseeable funding levels is to press again for tuition sensitivity in the Pell Grant award formula and to reduce or at least freeze the amount provided for living costs. Under a tuition sensitivity approach, the Pell Grant award formula would be divided into two components, one for tuition and one for living expenses. Such a change would allow for increases in the maximum award within existing funding levels.

For example, a formula that recognized 25 percent of tuition and fees (in combination with a standard living cost of $2,000) would yield a maximum award of perhaps $2,800 at current levels of funding, rather than the $2,300 maximum provided under existing rules. This would increase awards for disadvantaged students attending virtually all private colleges as well as relatively high-priced public institutions. The same formula would produce awards for community college students lower than what they now receive, but roughly equivalent to what they received before the 1992 reauthorization, which had the effect of shifting a substantial amount of funds in their direction.[11]

One argument against introducing tuition sensitivity into the Pell Grant program is that it might encourage higher tuitions, therefore running counter to the notion that federal student aid policy should discourage colleges from raising their prices. But to the extent that tuition increases would not be matched on a dollar-for-dollar basis in the Pell Grant award, the potential for tuition increases would be reduced. Pell Grant tuition sensitivity would be different from the workings of the student aid programs in which a dollar of tuition increase potentially results in an additional dollar of aid eligibility.

■ Conference Discussion

Martin Kramer echoed a long-standing view of many higher education professionals when he said, "The most important reform you could make in existing programs is to increase the Pell grant maximum award." Some conferees thought that we really do not know how effective Pell Grants have been in increasing access, as opposed to simply providing subsidies without changing behavior. "We should look at the evidence about the effectiveness of Pell Grants," Sandy Baum said, "and make policy judgments based on the evidence, not just our emotional reactions to grants and loans." Notwithstanding this caution, the principal question before the conference was how Pell Grants can be made more effective during a period of unrelenting stringency in the domestic federal budget.

David Breneman noted that "we have a $6 billion program that is stuck at the $2,300 level and shows no signs of growing significantly. And as other costs move up, the $2,300 maximum keeps dwindling in significance to the point that it's almost an embarrassment. So maybe the game should be to look hard at other ways to spend $6 billion rather than following the current eligibility rules." Breneman said he and Fred Galloway of the American Council on Education (ACE) have been commissioned by the College Board to analyze such alternatives, using ACE's Pell Grant estimation model. They would be looking at a range of alternatives, Breneman said, and he encouraged the audience and others in the field to come up with ideas as well.

Breneman acknowledged there was a political judgment involved in undertaking such an exploration. He thought some observers in the higher education community might say "one shouldn't tinker with options," because doing so might have the

effect of cementing the funding level at $6 billion, instead of forc-
ing the amount upward over time. But he said the alternative risk
is that if the Pell Grant program does remain stuck and the maximum does not grow, the program itself could be jeopardized.
"There comes a point," Breneman suggested, "when college pres-
idents won't spend the plane fare to come here and speak on its
behalf. It's not the central issue for many advocates of higher education that it was ten years ago."

Breneman offered preliminary figures from early computer
runs on some of the options under consideration in the College
Board study. For example, if Pell Grants were sharply limited to
students with family incomes of $20,000 or less, the result would
be a saving of more than $1 billion. Taking the $1 billion and applying it across the board for the under-$20,000 population might
push the maximum award close to $2,800, though not up to the
authorized level. If proprietary trade schools were to be removed
from the program, there would be a similar saving of about
$1 billion. Directing Pell Grants only to freshmen and sopho-
mores—one version of frontloading—might save as much as
$2.5 billion annually.

Breneman underscored the point that these numbers were estimates subject to further revision. The final report on the study
would set out the alternatives in a value-free format, to spark discussion on the future of the Pell Grant program.

Maureen McLaughlin added that the Department of Education
was examining a range of alternatives for restructuring Pell
Grants, including more tuition sensitivity in the formula, treatment of living expenses versus educational costs, and treatment of
dependent versus independent students. The department's review
is not restricted to "cost savers"; it is also looking at "cost shift-
ers" that might make the Pell Grant program more effective in
reaching the people who should be targeted.

James White of The Access Program in Lorain, Ohio, said he
was struck by the fact that nothing had been said in the entire
day's discussion about the federal methodology of need analysis
and whether it is the best way to determine eligibility for Pell
Grants as well as other aid programs. White's comment and audience reaction to it suggested that many conferees believe that the
federal methodology for determining family and student expected

contributions is unsatisfactory. White urged that this issue be included among the program parameters examined in the Breneman study.

Should federal policies take greater cognizance of state tuition and aid policies or encourage states to move in certain policy directions?

Although most states incorporate Pell Grants into the calculation of eligibility for their student aid programs, federal student aid policies and programs largely ignore the existence of state aid. In addition, the tuitions charged by public institutions (which are largely a function of state funding policies) are viewed as a given in the federal aid formulas.

This tradition of benign neglect on the part of the federal government could continue unabated were it not that so many things are happening at the state level that deserve a closer look by federal policymakers. For example, recent double-digit percentage increases in tuition and fees at public institutions mean that students attending them are borrowing more than ever before, thus contributing to the grant/loan imbalance. These rapid tuition increases were caused by the inability of states to sustain their funding commitments to public institutions during the most recent recession. Should the federal government recast its policies to reflect or influence state tuition and funding decisions?

A number of far-reaching proposals have been made regarding how federal and state responsibilities for funding postsecondary education and training should be divided. These proposals deserve a full airing, because the current division of responsibilities seems ill suited to handle future funding needs. Before she joined the leadership of the Office of Management and Budget in the Clinton administration, Alice Rivlin argued in her book *Reviving the American Dream* that the current split in responsibilities between the federal and state governments should be reassessed in a number of functional areas, including education and training. Rivlin suggested, for example, that the federal government might fully absorb the responsibility for health care, thus relieving the states of that increasingly large drain on their budgets. In exchange, Rivlin suggested placing more financial responsibility on the states for education and training, among other activities.[12]

McPherson and Schapiro took a sharply different tack in *Keeping College Affordable*. They argued that the federal government should assume more, not less, responsibility for the financing of higher education, through a substantial increase in the funding of the Pell Grant program. This infusion of federal funds would relieve state governments of the responsibility they have traditionally borne for providing general operating support of public institutions. The authors suggest that the Pell Grant program should be expanded to protect disadvantaged students from the higher tuitions that would result when hardpressed state governments reduce their allocations to public colleges.

The appeal of the McPherson and Schapiro plan and similar proposals is that the states would find resources freed up by virtue of having the federal government foot a bigger portion of the higher education bill through an expanded Pell Grant program. But the snag in this approach is that there is no readily apparent way to shift the state resources freed up by higher tuitions to help the federal government pay for a much larger Pell Grant program. With federal deficits as large as they are, doubling or tripling the funding for a federal program currently under so much scrutiny and criticism does not seem likely.

Between these extremes, a variety of alternative arrangements might result in more gradual and politically feasible shifts in responsibilities. For example, introducing tuition sensitivity into the Pell Grant formula would be one vehicle for federal policy influence on the states, without producing the wholesale shift in responsibilities envisioned in more radical proposals. Another idea that has been periodically floated since the early 1970s is to expand the old State Student Incentive Grants (SSIG) program, perhaps folding in some or all Pell Grant funds to create a much larger federal-state matching arrangement.

All of these proposals, and any others that would change how postsecondary education and training is paid for, must address where the funds to support these efforts would come from and how they would be financed.

—President Clinton and others in his administration including Labor Secretary Reich have broached the possibility of a payroll tax on employers to the extent they do not provide training to their employees. There is a nice logic in having employers pay for the benefit of having a better trained work force. But increased taxes are not a popular topic in the 1990s no matter how valid the use of funds generated might be.

—Before joining the Clinton administration, Alice Rivlin suggested a national sales tax in which the revenues would be shared by the states.[13] A national sales tax or value-added tax could be collected by the federal government on behalf of the states and distributed based on some formula that would provide some equalization. If such a tax were extended to services (which are now often exempt from state taxation), it could represent a new and significant source of revenue to support education. However, education would have to compete with other potential claims on such revenue, including health care, welfare reform, and law enforcement.

■ Conference Discussion

A number of conferees envisioned a "Super SSIG" program to bring federal and state policies into alignment for more effective support of higher education.

James Mingle called for expanded matching grants to the states for need-based student assistance. He suggested that to qualify for such federal matching grants, states should be required to allow portability of their grants so that students could use them to attend institutions in other states, and maintain fiscal effort in support of need-based student aid equal to or greater than increases in public sector tuition in the home state. Thus, if tuition goes up, student aid based on need would be available to meet those additional costs, and needy students would be held harmless.

Gordon Davies, director of the Virginia Council of Higher Education, suggested that this may be an idea whose time has come. "Enrollment growth in the United States will happen around the cup of the southern states," Davies said. "It starts about in Virginia and goes down the East Coast and across the center and up the West Coast. There are other states where enrollment growth isn't going to happen. In Virginia we are trying to figure out how to handle 80,000 more students on a base of 300,000 in the next ten years. So we are talking about using the capacity in other states for a highly mobile population. One problem we would have is making our financial aid programs mobile."

Davies went on to suggest: "Take the SSIG money and take the Pell Grant money and put it out there for those states that match it with some maintenance of effort, as Jim Mingle described, and make it portable. This would attack two problems at once, one being student need and the other how we in that cup of states handle a tremendous amount of enrollment growth. Maybe it's that last piece [mobility] that makes a 25-year-old idea newly attractive."

The Super SSIG as proposed would strengthen incentives for states to focus more of their resources on student assistance. Within federal parameters, states would be encouraged over time to shift their funding of higher education from operating support of institutions to need-based student aid. Some argued that political pressures at the state level mirror those in Congress to have postsecondary aid reach an ever-larger portion of the middle class. But the goal of the Super SSIG, through federal guidelines, would be to ensure that state programs and policies provide access for lower-income and disadvantaged students, particularly through a continuation and expansion of need-based student assistance.

NOTES

1. Richard W. Moore, "Proprietary Schools and Direct Loans," *Select Issues in the Federal Direct Loan Program* (U.S. Department of Education, 1994); and Arthur M. Hauptman with Jamie P. Merisotis, *The College Tuition Spiral* (New York: Macmillan/American Council on Accreditation and the College Board, 1990).

2. Janet S. Hansen, ed., *Preparing for the Workplace: Charting a Course for Federal Postsecondary Training Policy* (National Academy Press, 1994).

3. Per student, however, those in vocational training typically receive less financial assistance than their peers who go to college. Students in collegiate programs are eligible for more assistance per capita for more years than individuals who participate in vocational training, which typically takes a much shorter time than academic courses of study. Students who graduate from college and enroll in advanced degree programs may receive federal student aid in the form of grants and loans for five to ten years, while contracts for vocational training rarely last more than a year.

4. Many of those who never secure productive employment will not be able to fully repay their student loan obligations; under current legislation, they will then have all or a portion of their debt forgiven after twenty-five years. This forgiveness feature has led some to suggest that income contingency may not reduce defaults as much as define them out of existence.

5. *America's Choice: High Skills or Low Wages!*, report of the Commission on the Skills of the American Workforce (Rochester, N.Y.: National Center on Education and the Economy, 1990).

6. Alice M. Rivlin, *Reviving the American Dream: The Economy, the States, and the Federal Government* (Brookings, 1992).

7. A straightforward definition of students who are not college ready would be those who, upon entering college, need to take what the institution categorizes as remedial or developmental courses.

8. Michael S. McPherson and Morton Owen Shapiro, *Keeping College Affordable: Government and Educational Opportunity* (Brookings, 1991).

9. *Making College Affordable Again*, final report of the National Commission on Responsibilities for Financing Postsecondary Education (Washington, February 1993).

10. Instead, the reduction in what middle-class families are expected to contribute has expanded the eligibility of students primarily for loans, not grants.

11. For another perspective on the effects of the 1992 legislation on community colleges, see *The Impact of Federal Financial Aid Policy Changes on Community College Students*, prepared by the Institute for Higher Education Policy for the Association of Community College Trustees (Washington, February 1995).

12. Rivlin, *Reviving the American Dream*.

13. Ibid.

Chapter 3

Conclusions:
Seeking Guideposts for Reform

Before summarizing points of consensus emerging from the conference, we first try to capture a broad divergence of attitude and opinion that surfaced throughout the day's discussion on certain cross-cutting issues. Some of the views excerpted here come from the transcript of the conference; others are drawn from letters and reflections we later received from participants.

Some of the divergence at the conference may have been attributable to what Sandy Baum described as a "disconnect" between economic theorists and financial aid practitioners in addressing the issue of paying for college. For example, she said, economists tend to argue that students should borrow to cover most of their costs, on the grounds that most of the benefits accrue to individuals in the form of higher earnings after college. In the economist's view, if the rate of return is not high enough to permit repayment, then the investment must not be a good one. Meanwhile, many financial aid administrators are more concerned that students may be forced into borrowing because grant aid is unavailable, and they could therefore be overburdened with debt later on.

Baum called for a middle ground of both the "hard heads" of economists and the "soft hearts" of financial aid officers. "Too much dependence on loans will be a barrier to access, particularly for certain disadvantaged groups. On the other hand, borrowing is perfectly reasonable for the great majority of students."

DIVERGENCE OF VIEWS

Participants in the conference diverged on a number of broad issues of policy and strategy, particularly on the relative importance of restructuring the aid system versus providing more funding for existing programs.

A premise of the paper that was prepared for the conference as well as of this book is that existing federal student aid programs have not been as effective as they could and should be in achieving many of the policy goals set out in legislation and espoused by policymakers. A counterpoint voiced by many during the conference was that the existing program structure is essentially sound—the programs do work but simply need more funding to achieve policy goals. "It's not broke; don't fix it," some seemed to be arguing.

This point of view was best summarized by Bruce Johnstone, professor of education at the State University of New York at Buffalo and former chancellor of the State University of New York, in comments he was invited to make to conclude the conference. "I think we fuss too much," Johnstone said. "Our system may look strange and might not be replicated were we to start again. . . . But we should stop fussing out of the notion that some hitherto undiscovered restructuring plan can somehow make it all right and we'll go home happier with aid programs that are better funded and better able to be explained."

For all the faults of the student aid programs, Johnstone continued, and for all the faults in how we provide higher education in this country, America still has the best higher education system in the world. Student aid programs have helped create college participation rates that would have been unimaginable not that long ago. Johnstone went on to say that "serious tinkering" seems a more appropriate policy response at this juncture than leveling the existing system and starting fresh.

Other conferees expressed related sentiments. Some worried that if the higher education community advances proposals for restructuring, the result might be to reinforce doubts about current programs and thereby further jeopardize their funding.

Some conferees also were concerned that a preoccupation with problems in the existing system might obscure or further erode the primary mission of the aid programs: namely, assuring access for students who otherwise could not afford postsecondary education.

Humphrey Doermann captured this sentiment when he wrote that "relatively little attention and focus [in the paper and during the discussion] was put on the original legislative purposes underlying the

Higher Education Act of 1965. . . . If lack of money was a barrier to access and reasonable choice, need-based public aid would attempt to lower or remove the barrier. Families and students still had to contribute; but after reasonable contribution was made, government and colleges would do the rest." Doermann continued, "The principal purpose the legislative architects of the mid-1960s struggled for is the purpose that, most of the time, eroded as the increments of change worked through the Reagan, Bush, and Clinton years. That single, major stark reality did not (I thought) have much prominence at the Brookings discussions."

In a similar vein, Tom Mortenson, publisher of *Postsecondary Education OPPORTUNITY*, urged that policymakers not dwell on restructuring when the fundamental problem is underfunding of the programs. "Yes, it is important that we make sure that currently allocated funds are well spent on high priorities for policy. But all the [restructuring] in the world cannot make $5 billion work like the $20 billion needed to restore college affordability. . . . We are only rearranging the deck chairs on the *Titanic* if we limit our consideration to different allocations of the current level of appropriation. That misses the question of the adequacy of the funding for needs presented by students and the social benefits that might be expected were funding expanded."

A counterpoint to this view came from Sandy Baum, who wrote: "Dollars don't seem to be the fundamental explanation for the different college participation rates of young people from different socioeconomic backgrounds. . . . Much of the solution has to occur long before college decision time. Rethinking financial aid problems is important. Improved need analysis, a simpler application process, clear distinction between the need for liquidity and the need for subsidy, and increased emphasis on the parental role in financing college are all important. But none of these are likely to solve the basic social problems we are facing."

Another concern related to the issue of funding was that the higher education community needs to do a better job of documenting and publicizing the economic value of the postsecondary education and training that students receive. Rather than focusing on reform and redesign, a number of conference participants urged using the "returns-to-education" argument to bolster support for student aid. Several speakers noted that the postwar experience, especially in the

1980s, has been that postsecondary training yields positive rates of return to individuals and the economy, with the returns rising as more education is achieved.

For example, Thomas Kane asked, "If the rate of return on an investment in any form of postsecondary education and training is uniformly rising, shouldn't we view this as a good investment worthy of public taxpayer dollars?" Kane went on to question the "source of pessimism about how the system's working. The evidence is that the payoff on average for postsecondary students—even for people not finishing an associate's degree—is positive."

Maureen McLaughlin responded that these returns, while positive, are relatively small. "Average means some people do better, some do worse. . . . Even if there is a return to some college attendance, there is more of a return to completion."

Other conferees picked up on the theme of economic returns, urging that the education community needs to make a stronger case for stepping up federal and state investment in higher education. National policy, they said, should strive to give high-quality postsecondary training to as many students as possible. It should also assure that they have the opportunity to move logically upward from vocational training to a two-year associate's degree or to four-year education and beyond.

In response to this range of comments, we agree that inadequate appropriations and erosion of the purchasing power of available aid surely limit the effectiveness of the federal programs. We also agree that the education community must sustain and strengthen the case for investment in postsecondary training through student aid.

The difficulty, of course, is that in today's political and budgetary environment, there is intense competition for discretionary resources, and more funding for student aid is far from an easy sell. Student aid is unlikely to be pushed ahead of front-burner national priorities such as health care, welfare reform, and the like. Additional support for student aid is still more unlikely, to the extent that policymakers lack confidence that the aid programs are assuring students access to a quality education and success in completing their education.

In addition, we believe it is important to understand that the positive returns on postsecondary education over the past fifteen years have been more a function of the decline in real wages of those who did not continue past high school than of increasing returns for those who go to college. Thus we should not assume that postsecondary education will necessarily continue to produce positive economic returns, as was implied at the conference.

There also may be a pitfall in the argument that since there is a wage premium now attached to a college education, public policies should encourage more and more people to go to college. In the extreme case, if everyone went to college, there would be no wage premium for college graduates. Somewhere far short of a 100 percent college participation rate, this wage premium begins to disappear.

Finally, the question remains whether the mechanisms now used to help students finance education beyond high school are the best way to encourage such valuable education and training. That is, one could agree that postsecondary educational experience produces positive individual and societal returns yet still conclude that current aid programs are not the most efficient or effective ways to encourage students to continue their education. This is our starting point in arguing for the need for further changes in the federal student aid system.

POINTS OF AGREEMENT

Although conferees had mixed views on the need for restructuring and sometimes sharp divisions on specific proposals for reform, they also found significant common ground. The conference was not designed to marshall consensus (or to be strictly representative of all postsecondary education and training), yet people from quite different backgrounds and with highly variable sets of interests seemed to come together on some important points and principles during the course of the day.

The following are broad points of agreement that might serve as guideposts for future conversations on the direction of national efforts to equalize quality postsecondary educational opportunities for all.

Federal policies should emphasize student retention and persistence as much as access. A widely shared concern at the conference was that student aid programs seem to do a much better job of getting students into school than ensuring that they stay in school and receive their degrees. Access has been the touchstone of federal student aid policy for the past quarter-century; as a result, the aid programs are not as well suited to promoting persistence as they are to facilitating initial entry into the system. Future efforts should identify strategies that have a better chance of encouraging retention and persistence, especially among students who are economically and academically at risk.

Federal student aid programs should rely less on regulations and provide more incentives to ensure proper behavior by students as well as institutions. Throughout the course of the day, participants pointed to the lack of incentives—or to perverse incentives—in the current student aid system. One reason students may take longer to complete their course of study is that student aid policies do not encourage degree completion. Institutions also have little incentive for seeing that their aid recipients stay in school and complete their degrees. There was strong support for building incentives for both students and institutions into the aid system to encourage retention and degree completion as well as other key policy objectives.

Fraud and abuse should be dealt with separately from improving the overall quality of postsecondary education and training. A number of conference participants indicated that efforts to ferret out fraud and abuse in the system too often overlap with activities aimed at improving the overall quality of institutions. To reduce such confusion, it was suggested that fraudulent schools should not be treated in the same manner as honest schools having difficulty in providing quality education and training. To put this distinction into practice, the processes that federal and state governments undertake to prevent fraud and abuse should be different from those aimed at ensuring higher quality throughout all postsecondary education.

Regulatory policies should differentiate among postsecondary sectors and types of institutions. For years there has been discussion in the education community about whether students in proprietary trade schools should be eligible for aid programs that are different and separate from those available to students attending more traditional colleges and universities. Although the conference did not produce consensus in support of separate programs, there *was* considerable interest in differential regulatory solutions. Thus, different rules and regulations might apply to various types of institutions, all within the same legislative and programmatic framework. This question of differential treatment extends beyond the issue of how to address the problem of the trade school sector. For example, there was general support at the conference for identifying consistently high-performing institutions and rewarding them with a measure of regulatory relief not accorded borderline institutions.

Federal student aid policies should take greater cognizance of state tuition and student aid policies.   There seemed to be general support at the conference for bringing federal and state financing policies into broad alignment for more effective support of equity and quality in higher education. Though there was not necessarily consensus on how federal-state linkages might be forged, expanded federal matching of state need-based student grants—what some called a "Super SSIG"— attracted interest as an idea whose time may have come.

Finally, the goals of the federal aid programs need to be articulated more clearly.   A number of conference participants remarked on the diffuse, something-for-everyone aspect of federal student aid policies as they have evolved over time. Legislative and policy goals have not been sharply defined and clearly articulated. Although this is no doubt true of just about every domestic policy area, that lack of uniqueness makes it no less important for those making federal policy in postsecondary education and training to be clear about what they are trying to accomplish. To the extent that policy goals can be more clearly pinned down, the success of aid programs will be enhanced.

None of these suggested policy directions would vastly alter the "landscape" of higher education finance described by Frans J. de Vijlder. How we pay for college in America is likely to remain an untidy affair, reflecting our nation's diversity and our traditions of federalism. But these points of agreement can serve as guideposts for ongoing reform—a framework for future policy debates aimed at improving a system vital to the country's economic future and continued promise of opportunity.

Conference Panelists and Speakers

(with their affiliations at the time of the conference)

Sandy Baum
Associate Professor and Chair
Department of Economics
Skidmore College

André Bell
Dean of Enrollment
Bentley College

Stephen Blair
President
Career College Association

David Breneman
Professor of Education
Harvard University

Charles Clotfelter
Vice Provost for Academic Programs
Duke University

Dolores Cross
President
Chicago State University

Ronald Ehrenberg
Irving M. Ives Professor of
Industrial & Labor Relations and
* Economics*
Cornell University

Lawrence E. Gladieux
Executive Director for Policy
* Analysis*
The College Board

Janet Hansen
Senior Staff Officer and Study
* Director*
National Academy of Sciences

Arthur M. Hauptman
Consultant
Washington, D.C.

Bruce Johnstone
Professor of Education
State University of New York,
* Buffalo*

Thomas Kane
Visiting Fellow
The Brookings Institution

Martin Kramer
Consultant
Berkeley, Calif.

David Longanecker
Assistant Secretary for
* Postsecondary Education*
U.S. Department of Education

Bruce MacLaury
President
The Brookings Institution

Maureen McLaughlin
Special Assistant to the Assistant
* Secretary for Postsecondary*
* Education*
U.S. Department of Education

James R. Mingle
Executive Director
State Higher Education Executive
   Officers

David Pierce
President
American Association of Community
   Colleges

Donald M. Stewart
President
The College Board

Jane Wellman
Senior Associate
Institute for Higher Education Policy

Other Participants

(with their affiliations at the time of the conference)

Clifford Adelman
U.S. Department of Education

Marsha Adler
American Association of University Professors

Scott Anthony
U.S. News & World Report

Henry Aaron
Director, Economic Studies Program The Brookings Institution

David Baime
American Association of Community Colleges

Edwin Below
Wesleyan University

Ernst Benjamin
American Association of University Professors

Jim Belvin
Duke University

Robert Berdahl
University of Maryland

Della Berlanga
Corpus Christi (Texas) Independent School District

Robert Biehl
U.S. Department of Education

John A. Blackburn
University of Virginia

Theodore L. Bracken
Consortium on Financing Higher Education

Stan C. Broadway
North Carolina State Education Assistance Authority

James M. Brodie
American Association of University Professors

Steven Brooks
Wake Forest University

Kenneth B. Brown
The College Board

Jeneva Burroughs
Institute for Higher Education Policy

Thomas A. Butts
University of Michigan

Patrick Callan
California Higher Education Policy Center

Mark Cannon
Coalition for Student Loan Reform

Deborah Carter
American Council on Education

Kristine Castagnola-Thomas
U.S. Department of Education

Walter C. Cathie
Carnegie Mellon University

Daniel S. Cheever Jr.
American Student Assistance Corporation

Dan Chenok
Office of Management and Budget

John B. Childers
The College Board

George Chin
City University of New York

Alan Cohen
The College Board

Patricia Coye
Pomona College

Della Cronin
Clohan & Dean

John K. Curtice
State University of New York

Bob Davidson
U.S. Department of Education

Gordon K. Davies
State Council of Higher Education for Virginia

Jerry S. Davis
Student Loan Marketing Association

Charles Devarics
Black Issues in Higher Education

Humphrey Doermann
The Bush Foundation

Sally Donahue
Harvard Law School

Elaine El-Khawas
American Council on Education

Marcus Ellen
Office of Congressman Major Owens

Lawrence W. Feinberg
National Assessment Governing Board

Joni Finney
California Higher Education Policy Center

Brian Fitzgerald
Advisory Committee on Student Financial Assistance

Sarah Flanagan
National Association of Independent Colleges and Universities

Kathryn M. Forte
Whittier College

Jon W. Fuller
National Association of Independent Colleges and Universities

Carol H. Fuller
National Institute of Independent Colleges and Universities

Gregory Fusco
Columbia University

Fred Galloway
American Council on Education

Janice Gams
The College Board

Larry Gold
American Federation of Teachers

Daniel Goldenberg
U.S. Department of Education

Salomon Gomez
U.S. Department of Education

Jack Gorman
Colorado Student Loan Program

Allison Gray
Institute for Higher Education Policy

Judy Grew
Office of Management and Budget

Anna M. Griswold
Pennsylvania State University

Samuel Halperin
American Youth Policy Forum

John Hamilton
National Association of State Universities and Land-Grant Colleges

Matt Hamilton
University of Oklahoma

Hal Higginbotham
The College Board

William C. Hiss
Bates College

Mary Lee Hoganson
University of Chicago Laboratory High School

Robert P. Huff
The Hoover Institute Stanford University

Janet C. Hunter
Knox College

Samuel M. Kipp, III
California Student Aid Commission

Michael Johanek
The College Board

Charles H. Karelis
U.S. Department of Education

Kevin Keeley
National Association of College Admissions Counselors

Jacqueline King
The College Board

Laura Greene Knapp
Consultant
Arlington, Va.

Ruth Lammert-Reeves
Georgetown Law Center

Suzanne Lawrence
U.S. Department of Education

John Lee
JBL Associates

Brett E. Lief
National Association of Independent Colleges and Universities

James L. Lincoln
Grinnell College

Lynn Mahaffie
U.S. Department of Education

Stan Maliszewski
Omaha Public Schools

Dennis J. Martin
Washington University

Dallas Martin
*National Association of Student
    Financial Aid Administrators*

Laudelina Martinez
*Hispanic Association of Colleges and
    Universities*

Westina Matthews
Merrill Lynch

Patricia McAllister
Educational Testing Service

Barry McCarty
Lafayette College

Roberta Merchant
The College Board

Jamie P. Merisotis
Institute for Higher Education Policy

James M. Montoya
Stanford University

Eleanor S. Morris
*University of North Carolina at
    Chapel Hill*

Thomas G. Mortenson
*Postsecondary Education
    OPPORTUNITY*

Walter H. Moulton
Bowdoin College

Leo W. Munson
Texas Christian University

Susan Murphy
Cornell University

Leslie Mustain
Office of Management and Budget

Nan Nixon
Harvard University

Don Nolan
*New York State Education
    Department*

Rhonda D. Norsetter
University of Wisconsin, Madison

Elaine Norvak
University of Michigan

Paul M. Orehovec
University of Miami

Sharon Thomas Parrott
DeVry Inc.

Gina Pearson
*National Association of Graduate
    and Professional Students*

Barbara Peterson
*Washington State Higher Education
    Coordinating Board*

Donald V. Raley
Dickinson College

Ken Redd
*National Association of Independent
    Colleges and Universities*

John R. Reeves
Student Loan Marketing Association

Deborah Reilly
*National Association of Independent
    Colleges and Universities*

John Reynders
Allegheny College

Constance Rhind
Congressional Budget Office

Lois D. Rice
The Brookings Institution

Eric D. Robertson
Georgetown University

Kenneth W. Rodgers
The College Board

Mary Ann Rowan
Loyola University Chicago

Joseph A. Russo
University of Notre Dame

Donald A. Saleh
Cornell University

William M. Schilling
University of Pennsylvania

Frank Schmidtlein
University of Maryland

Robert Seaver
The College Board

Mike Sherry
Education Daily

Bob Shireman
*Office of Senator Paul Simon
(D.-Ill.)*

Dave Simpson
Education Finance Council

Thomas P. Skelly
U.S. Department of Education

Joyce Smith
*National Association of College
Admissions Counselors*

Bruce Smith
The Brookings Institution

Pat Smith
Office of Management and Budget

Larry Soler
Association of American Universities

Wayne Sparks
University of Virginia

A. Clayton Spencer
*U.S. Senate Committee on Labor
and Human Resources*

Peter Stanley
Pomona College

Barry Wade Stevens
U.S. Department of Education

Jamienne Studley
U.S. Department of Education

Anne Sturtevant
Emory University

Jerome H. Sullivan
University of Colorado at Boulder

Claire Swann
University of Georgia

Cathy Thomas
University of Southern California

Steven Thorndill
University of Puget Sound

Becky Timmons
American Council of Education

Kenneth Tolo
U.S. Department of Education

Jo Ann Tooley
U.S. News & World Report

Barbara Tornow
Boston University

Nellie C. Vizcarrondo
*Puerto Rico Council on Higher
   Education*

Linda C. Waddell
Lane Community College

Benny Walker
Furman University

Leonard M. Wenc
Carleton College

James W. White
*The Access Program
Lorain, Ohio*

Philip Wick
Williams College

Margaret Williamson
*Presbyterian College—South
   Carolina*